Herbal
Handbook

Herbal Handbook

NYBG
EST 1891

51 Profiles in Words and Art
from the Rare Book and Folio Collections
of The New York Botanical Garden

CLARKSON POTTER/PUBLISHERS
NEW YORK

Contents

9 *Acknowledgments*

10 *Introduction*

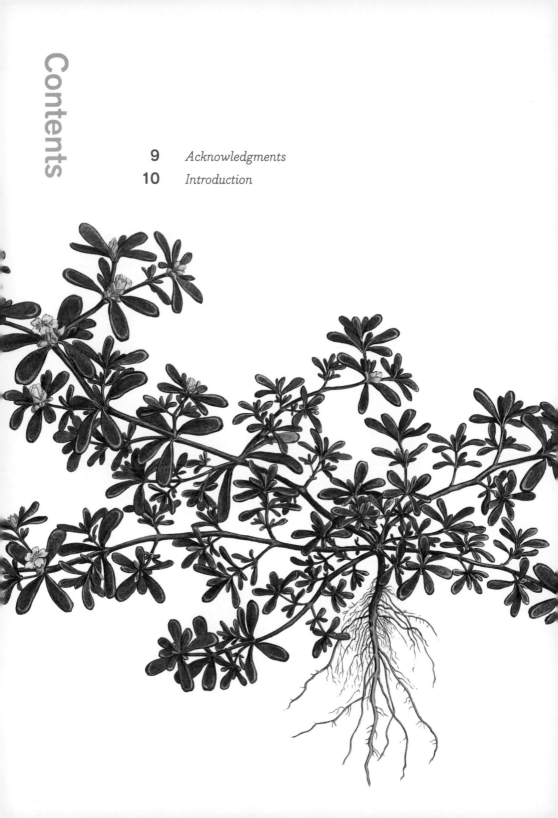

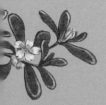

12 Basil

15 Bergamot

18 Borage

21 Calendula

24 Caraway

28 Catnip

31 Chamomile

34 Chervil

38 Chicory

42 Chives

45 Cilantro

48 Clary Sage

51 Clove Pink

54 Cornflower

57 Dandelion

61 Dill

64 Fennel

68 Fenugreek

71 Hollyhock

74 Horehound

77 Lavender

80 Lemon Balm

83 Lemon Verbena

86 Lovage

89 Mallow

92 Marjoram

95   Meadowsweet

98   Mustard

101   Nasturtium

104   Oregano

107   Parsley

110   Peppermint

113   Pineapple Weed

117   Purslane

120   Rhubarb

124   Rosemary

128   Saffron

132   Sage

136   Salsify

139   Savory

143   Scented Geranium

146   Sesame

149   Soapwort

152   Sorrel

155   Spearmint

158   Stinging Nettle

161   Sweet Woodruff

164   Tarragon

167   Thyme

170   Wild Violet

173   Yarrow

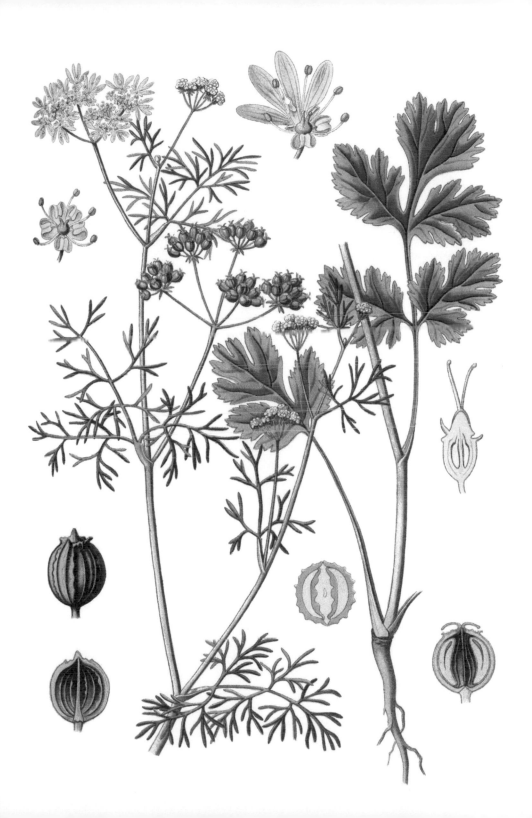

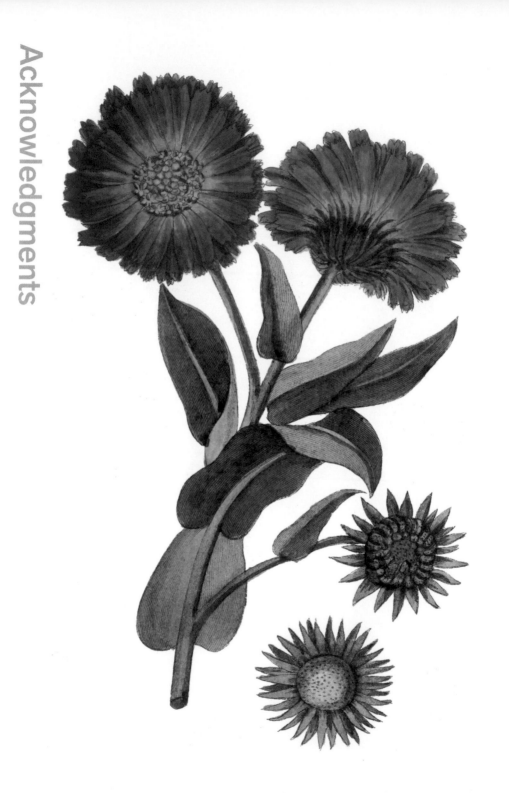

Acknowledgments

Herb profiles written by Rachel Federman

Research provided by Stephen Sinon, William B. O'Connor Curator of Special Collections, Research, and Archives at The New York Botanical Garden.

Seasonal Display Cocktail (Borage), Carawrye Cocktail (Caraway), Root and Stem Cocktail (Chicory), Rock and Rye Cocktail (Horehound), Jewel Mix Cocktail (Nasturtium), Long Red Jacket Cocktail (Rhubarb), These Hours are Golden Cocktail (Saffron), and Mai-Wineless Punch (Woodruff) courtesy James Freeman

Calendula Cleanser, Chamomile Eye Therapy Compress, and Yarrow Bath courtesy Andrea Candee, MH, MSC

Minty Bourbon Citrus Cocktail (Spearmint) courtesy Kim Keller

White Bean Soup and Japanese-style White Mustard recipes courtesy Raquel Pelzel

Note to reader:
People have used herbal remedies for thousands of years. But remember, as with all foods you ingest, anything applied to your skin may provoke an allergic reaction, so if you have any medical condition you should consult with your health care professional before using the calendula cleanser, or the chamomile eye therapy compress, or any of the herbal remedies mentioned in the Usage sections of the herb profiles.

Fairy clock. Lion's teeth. Little dragon. Eye of the star. Calendula. Meadowsweet. Juno's tears. These plants conjure enchanted worlds, brighten our gardens, enrich our meals, heal our bodies, freshen our air, soothe us before sleep. If one wants to believe in magic, one might do well to begin with the study of herbs.

From the tomb of Tutankhamun to medieval kitchen gardens to suburban lawns, herbs are everywhere, and have been with us for thousands of years. Archaeological remains indicate that as long as there have been people on this planet, there have been plants that supported them. Their use predates any surviving written records we have. At the cross-section of botany, medicine, history, natural history, the culinary arts, holistic healing, and, of course gardening, herbs have a stunning range of aromas, flavors, and applications. On our tables, at our weddings, in our skin care regimens and in our sacred rituals, they mark the seasons and connect us to the past. They give us flowers and essential oils. Some revitalize our spirits; others help relieve anxiety and settle us down. They can be sewn into dream pillows, cut fresh for bouquets, rubbed on the scalp to invigorate the hair, or grown to turn your lawn into a fairy-tale cottage garden.

What makes an herb an herb? The definition is two-branched. Botanically an herb is defined as a plant that produces seeds but does not develop a woody stem. But an herb is also defined as any plant with leaves, flowers, seeds, stems or roots that can be used for seasoning, medicine, or perfume.

In this book you'll find herbs in Sanskrit texts and Renaissance cookbooks, in Greek myths and Roman feasts, and lining the baby cribs of North American indigenous peoples. There's a hollyhock festival in Japan, lavender fields in Provence, Indian curries, Greek spanakopita, and ancient love potions. The simple entries—which all include a description, instructions for growing, and tips for usage—take you from marshes to rocky cliffs, across pastures, into woods, through cultivated fields, across oceans, and along the Silk Road. Some herbs are considered weeds, and others are precious and treasured, handpicked from plants that flower briefly, with blooms that fade quickly.

And because it's best to learn by doing, each herb profile includes a recipe or project using that herb. You'll see how they can be chopped into salads and soups, sautéed in oil, or used to flavor pasta, garnish punches, enhance baked goods, and steeped for a comforting tea. Whether you find them growing in the wild or cultivate them with care; whether you use them to transform your mood or your food, welcome the spring, or cheer up your living room, we're sure you'll enjoy learning about these plants and trying your hand at the recipes that follow. Despite a multiplicity of uses, you'll find herbs reassuring in their simplicity: they need water, and they (mostly) love the sun.

Basil

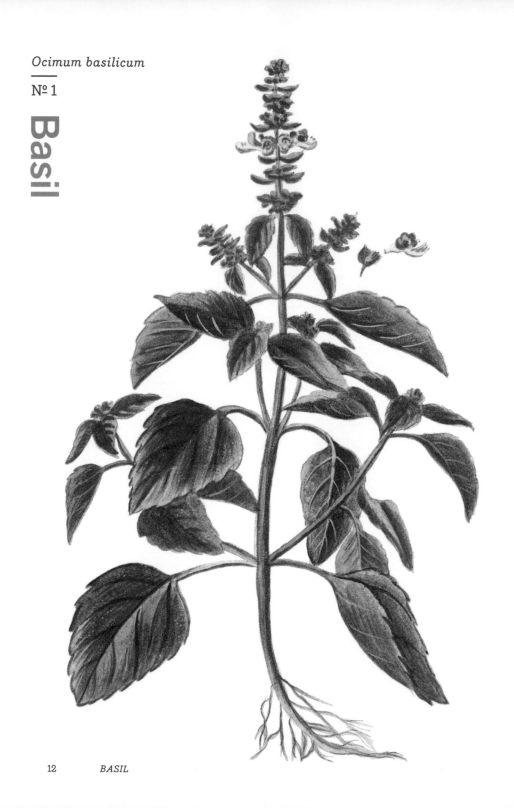

TO GROW

Basil grows easily in full sun and moist, well-drained soil. It can be sown indoors and transplanted outdoors or continue to be grown in containers indoors. Transplant seedlings from indoors after danger of frost has ended. Spread out so they are separated by at least 1 foot. Harvest in early morning. Produces leaves throughout the growing season. Use fresh or preserve in oil in the refrigerator.

USAGE

A favorite in Italian cuisine, basil is perhaps best known for its role in pesto. Combined with pine nuts, Parmesan cheese, garlic, and oil, it makes mouthwatering sauce, commonly served on pasta. It is also an essential ingredient in the Italian caprese salad, complemented by mozzarella and tomato. It can be combined with strawberries and a drizzle of sticky balsamic vinegar for a unique take on shortcake dessert.

Basil is in the same family as mint, along with rosemary and lavender. There are more than sixty species of basil. Sweet basil and Thai basil are the two main types, and sweet basil is the most common. Likely native to Asia and Africa, basil represented mourning to the ancient Greeks and was called *sileus phuton*, kingly herb. Today it is still sometimes called "king of herbs." Basil had a mixed reputation in medieval times. Some claimed it could cure scorpion bites. Others thought it was poisonous. In the seventeenth century, Nicholas Culpeper said it had a "virulent quality." At various points in history, it was called a "devil's plant." It is still associated with scorpions and the astrological sign Scorpio. Flowers are typically white.

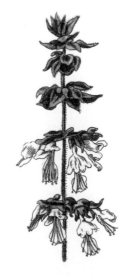

Tomato Basil Pesto

Tomatoes and basil are a marriage made in heaven. Use on roasted vegetables, pasta, or bulgur as a refreshing substitute for tomato sauce.

YIELD
———
Makes 2 cups pesto

  1 clove garlic
10 cherry tomatoes
 ⅓ cup pine nuts
 ⅓ cup grated Parmesan cheese
 ⅓ cup good olive oil
  3 cups tightly packed basil leaves
     Salt to taste

In a food processor, combine all ingredients except except the basil and pulse until smooth. When well combined, add the basil and pulse to incorporate.

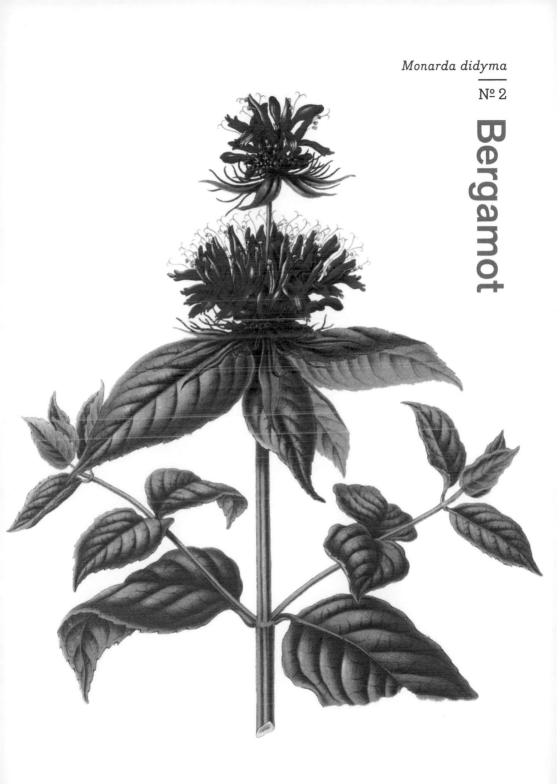

Bergamot

Bee Balm symbolizes good health, protection from illness, and prosperity.

TO GROW

Grow bergamot in full sun to partial shade, in well-drained soil. It tolerates a wide range of soils and will reach 2 to 4 feet. Pinching blooms will lengthen the summer flowering season. Be careful not to overwater because it is prone to mildew. Harvest leaves before flowering, and harvest the flowers immediately after they bloom.

USAGE

Both leaves and petals can be used to flavor and garnish lemonades, punches, wines, and jellies. Try flowers as garnish for sangria. Leaves can be added to salads, herb butters, and vegetable dishes. Bergamot pairs well with mint and can be enjoyed on fruit, especially strawberries. It is sometimes added to fish and seafood. It is valued in aromatherapy and its dried leaves make a nice addition to potpourri and sachets. It is used as a balm for bee stings, hence the nickname bee balm. When grown as an ornamental plant it attracts hummingbirds, bees, and butterflies.

A perennial native to North America, bergamot is also called bee balm, high balm, low balm, mountain balm, Oswego tea, horsemint, wild bergamot, and mountain mint. The Oswego tribe made a drink with the red variety of bergamot (*Monarda didyma*). When the colonists boycotted British tea, they turned to the bergamot drink made by native people as an alternative. The Iroquois and Tewa tribes also valued the herbaceous plants.

The genus name honors Spanish botanist Nicolás Monardes, who identified the plant in the sixteenth century. Its citrusy fragrance resembles that of the bergamot orange fruit (*Citrus bergamia*), which is mainly grown in Italy and used in Earl Grey tea. But the herb bergamot is not an ingredient in the tea. Flowers depend on the variety, ranging from pink to lavender to a brilliant red in the scarlet variety. A lovely addition to a cottage garden.

Bergamot Iced Tea

YIELD

Makes 2 cups iced tea

8   fresh bergamot leaves (picked in early
    morning, when the oils are strongest)
1   teaspoon sugar or to taste
2   cups water

Place bergamot leaves in a medium-size heatproof
bowl. Sprinkle the sugar over them.

Bring the water to a boil. Pour over the leaves and steep
for several hours. Strain into a heatproof jar and chill.
To serve, pour over ice.

Note: If the bergamot alone is too strong, mix
with the same amount of another brewed tea
of your choice.

Borage officinalis

№ 3

Borage

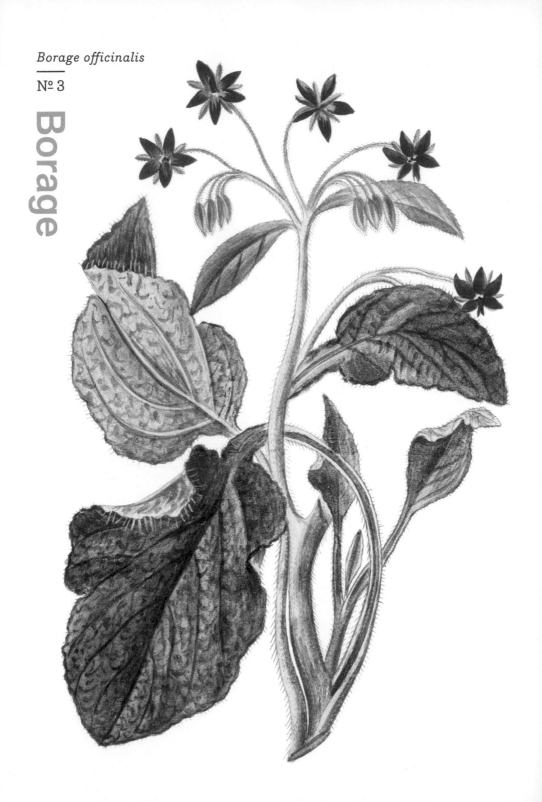

In the Victorian language of flowers, borage stands for bluntness.

TO GROW

Reaching 2 to 3 feet, borage grows easily from seed. Choose a location with full sun, and be sure to keep soil moist and well drained. Harvest leaves at any time. They're best consumed fresh, as dried versions lose flavor. The flowers can be harvested and enjoyed fresh as well.

USAGE

Try sautéing the leaves in garlic, along with the stems. Stems can also replace celery in potato salad. The flowers make an attractive edible garnish. Iced borage tea, enhanced with honey and lemon juice, makes a refreshing drink in warm weather. Crystallized foliage is used in candies, and a blue dye can be produced from the flowers. Borage will also attract bees to your garden.

Native to the Mediterranean, this self-seeding annual is also called bee bread or star flower (sometimes written as one word—starflower). *Bugloss* is also very common. The star-shaped flowers are sky blue and hang in drooping clusters; the leaves are gray-green. The plant has a smell and taste reminiscent of cucumber. Both leaves and stalks have a bristly fuzz that helps shield the plant from insects.

In the first century AD, Greek physician Pedanius Dioscorides mentioned a comforting drink made from borage. The Greeks made medicinal infusions from the herb, and Roman naturalist Pliny the Elder suggested it for curing hiccups. He authored the most extensive work on the natural world to have survived from ancient times. According to Pliny the Elder, borage was known as a *euphorosinum*, a plant that elicits a feeling of euphoria. The herb was valued by the Romans, who mixed both the flowers and leaves into wine. Some say nepenthe, the drug referenced by Homer, was this self-seeding herb, which leads to memory loss when steeped in wine. The Welsh name, *Ilanwenlys*, means herb of gladness.

Seasonal Display Cocktail

YIELD
___

Makes 1 cocktail

Borage is a classic summer cocktail ingredient.
It's an ingredient in Pimm's Cup No. 1 and
also part of its traditional garnish. The sweet
cucumber flavor of the leaves pairs perfectly with
gin, lemon, and other summery flavors, and the
starry blue flowers can be frozen into ice cubes
for a visual treat.

5 or 6	fresh borage leaves
1½	ounces London dry gin
½	ounce simple syrup
¾	ounce freshly squeezed lemon juice
4	ounces green tea, cooled

Gently muddle the borage in the bottom of a mixing
glass. Add the gin, simple syrup, lemon juice, and plenty
of ice, and stir until well chilled. Pour into a tall glass
over fresh ice, fill with the tea, and stir a few times to
mix. Garnish with a borage flower (after removing the
green leafy part of the flower, which can be prickly).

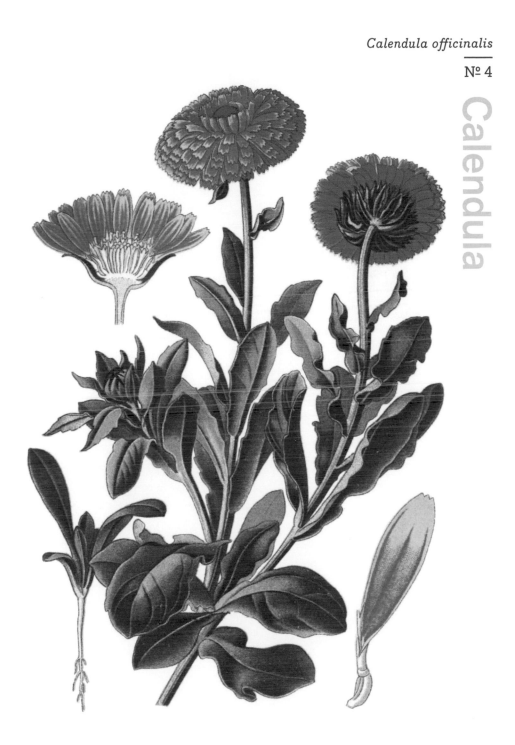

In India, calendula has become a symbol of thankfulness and serenity.

TO GROW

Calendula grows easily in full sun or partial shade. It likes well-drained soil, but can tolerate almost any kind. Plant seeds outside after danger of last frost has past. It will grow 18 to 24 inches and begins flowering in June. Flowers open during the day and close at night. Harvest flowers when the sun is out. Closed flower heads in the morning mean rain.

USAGE

Add the petals to salads, soups, breads, and risotto dishes. Can also be used to make tea and to color butter and cheese. The oil has moisturizing properties and is used for skin lotions and nourishing treatments, including facials. Used commercially to make a yellow dye. Some use calendula to treat burns.

Calendula is a member of the same family as the daisy. Native to the Mediterranean, Europe, and Egypt, it is also known as pot marigold, garden marigold, holligold, goldbloom, and Mary bud. Most of the fifteen to twenty species of calendula are called marigolds. Its long growing season may have given rise to the name—in some warmer climates it grows every month of the calendar year. The name *marigold* is also thought to relate to the Feast of the Annunciation of Mary, welcoming spring, hence Mary's gold. Ancient Roman authors Virgil and Pliny both mentioned calendula in their writings.

However, it is not the same as the marigold commonly found in gardens, which is part of the genus *Tagetes*. While calendulas are edible, with a mild, peppery taste, other *Tagetes* species should be avoided— unpleasantly bitter to the taste at best and, at worst, toxic. Calendula flowers are yellow or orange and open in the daytime, closing at night. In the Middle Ages, it was called "poor man's saffron." The herb has a long medicinal history extending from ancient times and was used as an antiseptic in the American Civil War and First World War.

Calendula Cleanser

Calendula's ability to soothe irritated and sensitive skin is well known. Try making a simple homemade facial cleanser by boiling 1 cup of fresh petals in 2 cups of milk.

Simmer for 30 minutes, then strain out the petals. Once cooled, massage into the face and neck. Rinse with warm water.

To lighten and brighten hair color, try rinsing with a tea brewed from the petals.

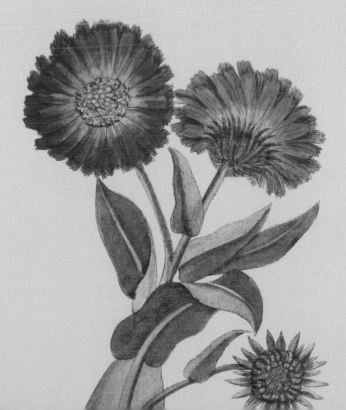

Caraway

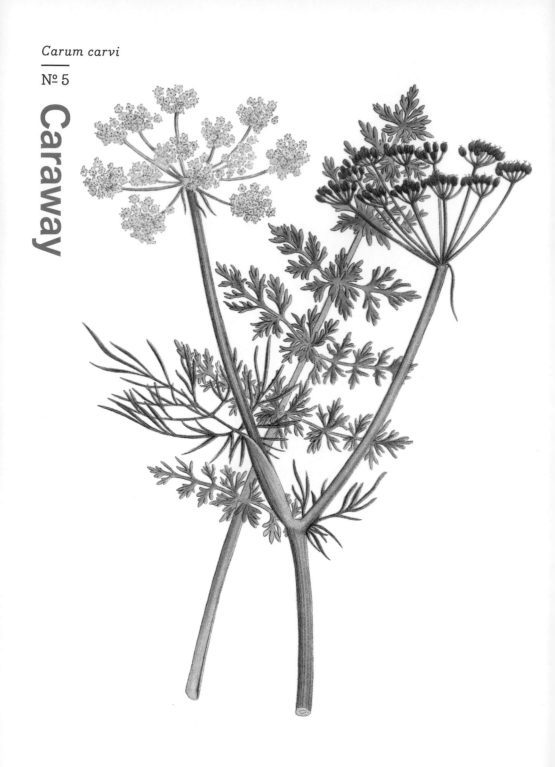

Caraway was used in love potions, and was once thought to protect things and even children from getting stolen or lost.

TO GROW

Caraway prefers full sun and well-drained soil. It doesn't transplant well; it is best grown from seed in moist soil. It will produce seeds in the second season. Harvest roots when the plant is young; leaves can be harvested at any time. Seeds are best after they turn brown, harvested in the morning before the dew dries. Seeds should be completely dried before being stored.

USAGE

Use the roots as you would parsnips or carrots. Add leaves to salads, soups, and stews or sauté with garlic and oil. Seeds pair well with cabbage, garlic, cheese, potatoes, and sausage dishes. Caraway is a common ingredient in pickles, in a German liquor known as kummel, and in aquavit, a Scandinavian spirit. It is essential to Jewish rye bread, pumpernickel, and Irish soda bread. During the Ramadan holiday in the Middle East, a pudding called meghli is made with caraway. It can be used to make tea, an ancient remedy for digestive ailments, and

A member of the parsley family, caraway is also known as Persian cumin, Roman cumin, meridian fennel, wild cumin, and *siya jeera*. Known for its licorice-like flavor, it is native to North Africa, Asia, and Europe. It is generally cultivated for its seeds, but has edible roots and leaves as well. Ancient Greek physician Dioscorides knew of caraway. A collection of fourteenth-century recipes called *The Forme of Cury* (thought to be compiled by the head chefs of Richard II) mentions caraway along with nutmeg, cardamom, and ginger.

is thought to have many medicinal benefits, including as an antiseptic and antihistamine. The oil is used for its fragrance in soaps and lotions. Caraway seeds are often chewed to freshen breath.

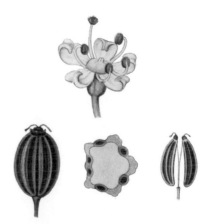

Carawrye Cocktail

Caraway may not be an obvious cocktail flavoring, but infused in rye whiskey, it invokes the taste of old-fashioned celery soda. Pair it with a classic Reuben.

YIELD
———
Makes 1 cocktail

- 1 ½   ounces Caraway-Infused Rye Whiskey (recipe follows)
- ¾   ounce freshly squeezed lemon juice
- ½   ounce Amontillado sherry
- ¼   ounce simple syrup

Fill a cocktail glass with ice and add all the ingredients. Stir until very cold, then strain into a chilled cocktail glass. Top, if desired, with 1 ½ ounces seltzer or soda water.

Caraway-Infused Rye Whiskey

1   cup rye whiskey (I used Rittenhouse)
½   ounce caraway seeds (about 2 tablespoons)

In a small skillet over medium heat, lightly toast the
seeds in a skillet until fragrant, about 1 minute. Remove
immediately and let them cool, then add to the whiskey
in a nonreactive container. Shake well and let stand.
Shake once a day and taste daily; the flavor will develop
within 2 to 3 days. Strain through a fine mesh strainer
and bottle. Keeps indefinitely.

Catnip

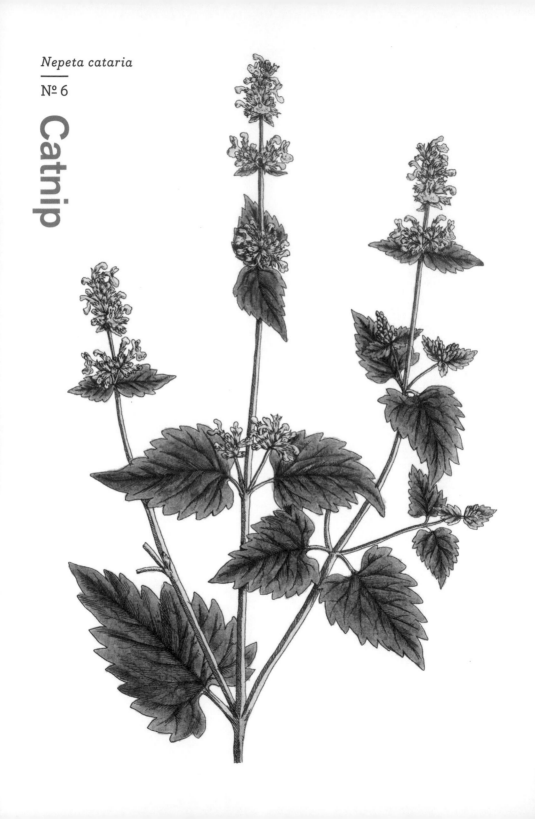

In the language of flowers, catnip means intoxication with love.

TO GROW

Preferring full sun and well-drained soil, catnip will reach 3 feet and can tolerate droughts. Grow from seeds or plants and protect from wandering cats. Be careful not to overwater. If growing for your cat, pick when plant blooms in the middle of summer. Cut from the bottom of the stem, then hang harvested stems upside down to dry, crushing leaves when they are fully dry.

USAGE

Catnip's most common usage is as a stimulant for cats, and it is commonly found in cat toys. When it comes to humans, catnip is most often used as a tea, although there are questions as to its safety for human consumption. Topically applied, catnip tea is said to be effective combatting dandruff. Catnip is also found as a flavoring in soups, sauces, and various drinks. Potpourri mixes sometimes include the aromatic herb. Catnip can also be used as a mosquito, deer tick, and rat repellent.

The perennial plant is a member of the mint family native to continental Europe, Asia, the Middle East, and Africa. Catnip is also known as catmint, catwort, or field balm. Its intense effect on cats is well known. What may be less familiar is its ability to attract butterflies. In late spring, clusters of lavender flowers appear. Catnip (or "nep," as it was called), was popular in the Middle Ages. It was grown in kitchen gardens and enjoyed fresh in salads and as a seasoning for meat.

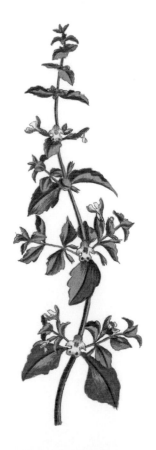

Sweet Sleep Herbal Sachet

If you have a cat, keep this away as lavender and lemon are toxic for cats.

   4 x 8-inch square muslin or cheesecloth
   Needle and thread
1 tablespoon dried catnip leaves
3 tablespoons dried lavender leaves
1 tablespoon dried sage leaves
1 tablespoon dried mint leaves
1 slice lemon peel (1 inch long)

Fold the cloth in half to create a 4-inch-square pocket. Stitch up two sides, leaving the top open. Mix the dried herbs in a small bowl and stuff into the pocket. Drop the lemon peel in and sew the opening shut. Place in a drawer to freshen.

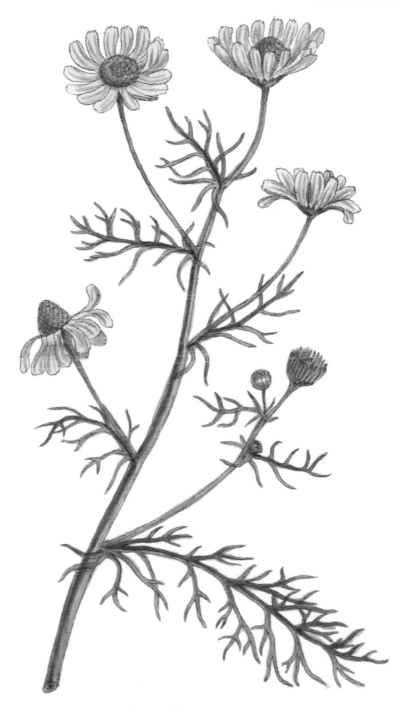

Matricaria recutita

№ 7

German Chamomile

In the Victorian language of flowers, chamomile represents patience through adversity.

TO GROW

Full sun or partial shade in a cool climate is best for chamomile, which cannot endure conditions that are too hot or dry. Grow from seeds or cuttings or, if you prefer, by dividing roots, and expect flowers to reach approximately 10 inches. Roman chamomile will spread easily and needs to be pruned. For German chamomile, an early spring planting of seeds close enough to the surface will allow the light necessary for growth. Keep soil moist and well drained.

USAGE

Popular as both a tonic and a relaxing drink, chamomile is often used for a calming tea. Steep dried flowers in water that is almost boiling, then add honey or another sweetener, lemon, and mint according to preference. Peppermint and chamomile also pair well in teas. Some alcoholic drinks draw on chamomile's apple flavor—such as Spanish sherry, a mixed drink with bourbon and honey—as well as some wheat beers. Avoid chamomile if allergic to aster plants, including ragweed.

There are two common varieties of chamomile in the family Asteraceae/Compositae: German and Roman. Both types resemble small daisies. German chamomile is an annual that produces more than one flower on separated stems. Roman chamomile is also called English chamomile, a reference to the fragrant lawns and tennis courts of chamomile enjoyed by the Elizabethans. Roman chamomile is a perennial often used for ground cover and to fill in small spaces in gardens. Both types can be brewed to make tea.

The name *chamomile* comes from two Greek words: *khamai*, meaning on the ground, and *melon*, which means apple. The plant's apple-like smell was noted by Pliny the Elder. The plant originated in Europe and West Asia and has been widely used, and often held sacred, since antiquity.

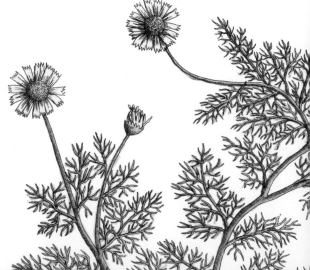

Chamomile Eye Therapy Compress

When eyes are red, sore, or irritated as a result of allergies, environmental pollutants, or fatigue, the anti-inflammatory properties of chamomile provide gentle relief in the form of compresses or eye drops.

For a compress: Pour 1 cup boiled distilled water (this can be purchased in health food stores, pharmacies, or supermarkets) over 2 teaspoons dried chamomile flowers. Steep and let cool until just warm, then strain. Dip a washcloth or cotton pads into the infusion, squeezing gently; apply over eyelids for 20 minutes.

Repeat 3 to 4 times a day, reheating the tea for a more soothing effect.

The tea may be stored in the refrigerator for 3 days.

GERMAN CHAMOMILE

Chamomile Eye Drop Therapy

Prepare the tea infusion as for the compress above and let cool.

Strain the fluid very well through layers of cheesecloth, a linen napkin, or a paper coffee filter. Pour into a dropper bottle and administer 1 to 2 drops in each eye, 3 to 4 times daily. The eye drops are good for 3 days if stored in the refrigerator.

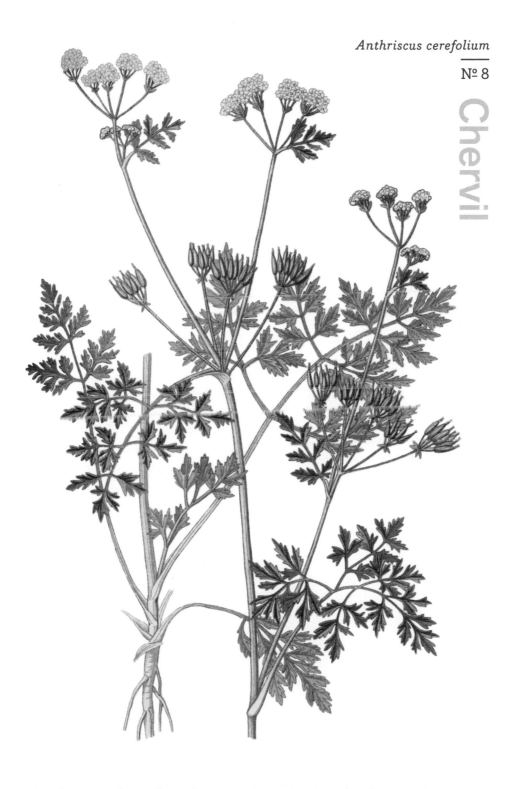

In the Victorian language of flowers, chervil symbolizes sincerity.

TO GROW

Grows well in partial shade, with moist soil and not too much heat. Will reach 2 feet. When planting, cover with only a thin layer of soil to allow access to light for germination. Harvest by picking leaves on the outside before the plant flowers.

USAGE

Along with parsley, chives, and tarragon, chervil is one of the ingredients in the classic French mixture *fines herbes*. Add to salads, sauces, scrambled eggs, and vegetable dishes. Try it in a lemon-butter sauce. It is especially nice with asparagus, and used often in cream sauces for fish and chicken. Add at the end of preparation, as chervil loses flavor with too much heat.

An annual herb popular in France, and native to Europe and the Caucasus, chervil is a member of the carrot family. It is also called garden chervil, French parsley, cicily, and sweet cicely. It resembles parsley, but in a lighter shade of green. The name comes from Greek *chairephyllon*, leaves of joy. The Romans treated chervil as a green vegetable. Although the plant is related to parsley and cilantro, the taste is closer to anise, fennel, and tarragon.

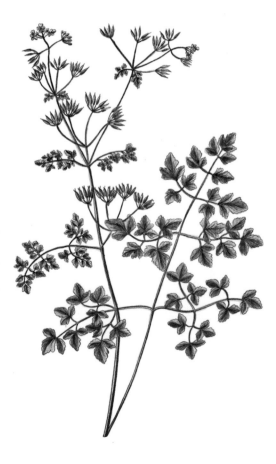

Chervil Omelet

The delicate anise flavor of chervil in this classic omelet perfectly complements the earthy Gruyère cheese.

YIELD
___

Serves 2

4 large eggs
1 tablespoon olive oil
¼ cup grated Gruyère cheese
¼ cup chopped chervil
Salt and freshly ground pepper to taste

In a medium-size bowl, whisk the eggs until frothy. Heat the olive oil in a nonstick skillet over medium heat. When it shimmers, pour in the beaten eggs and swirl to set. When the mixture is no longer runny, sprinkle in the Gruyère and chervil. Fold a third of the omelet over the center and do the same on the other side. Sprinkle with salt and pepper.

Serve with thinly sliced buttered toast.

Chicory

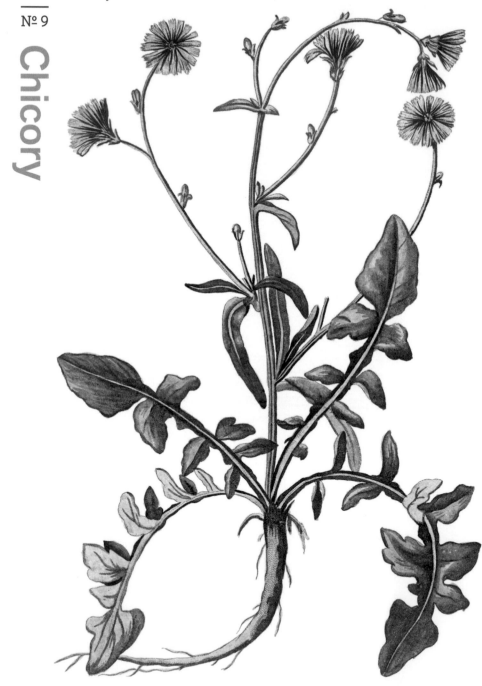

In the Victorian language of flowers, chicory symbolizes frugality.

TO GROW

Chicory prefers sun, is easy to grow in most soils, and requires little attention outside of watering in dry weather. May reach 2 to 5 feet and will bloom every 2 years.

USAGE

Spring and autumn are the best times to harvest wild chicory leaves. The heat of summer can produce bitterness. When harvesting in summer, blanch before cooking to reduce bitter flavor. Try sautéing young leaves with oil and garlic as you would spinach. Boiled chicory roots can be served like parsnips, with butter. A caffeine-free coffee substitute can be made from brewing ground roasted roots. It can also be mixed with coffee, adding a nutty flavor.

Chicory is also called blue sailors, blue daisy, blue dandelion, succory, coffeeweed, ragged sailors, wild endive, and sometimes cornflower. A thick-rooted perennial native to Eurasia, it flourishes along fields and roadsides, growing particularly well in limestone soils. The flower heads are pale sky blue or lavender and open only once and for a short time, starting in the morning and closing by midday. The beloved New Orleans coffee substitute is made from its long taproot.

Chicory's culinary history began at least as early as ancient Rome, and Pliny the Elder made note of its myriad benefits. Many varieties have been cultivated since that time, such as radicchio and Belgian endive. (A vegetable relative, endive is harvested for its leaves—frisée in its curly form—and otherwise called escarole.)

Root and Stem Cocktail

Chicory, the humble root of the fancy endive plant, is used as a coffee flavoring, so chicory syrup can fulfill a similar role as coffee liqueur, but with less alcohol. Here it is combined with Cynar, an Italian herbal liqueur, which has a similar warm, earthy flavor.

YIELD

Makes 1 cocktail

- **1** ounce bourbon
- **1** ounce aged rum
- **½** ounce Cynar
- **½** ounce Chicory Syrup (recipe follows)
- **1** dash orange bitters

Fill a mixing glass with ice and add all the ingredients. Stir to chill, then strain into a chilled cocktail glass.

Chicory Syrup

2 heaping teaspoons powdered chicory root
1 cup sugar

Heat 1 cup water to boiling; pour into a heatproof bowl.
Add 2 heaping teaspoons of powdered chicory root
and infuse for 5 minutes, or longer for more flavor.
Add 1 cup sugar and stir to dissolve. Strain through a
fine mesh strainer and cool completely. Store in the
refrigerator indefinitely.

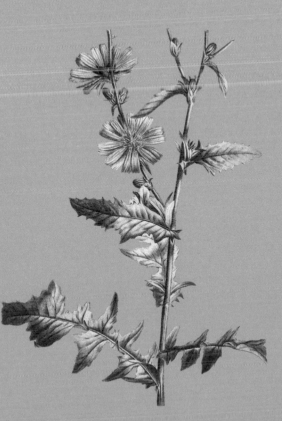

Allium schoenoprasum

№ 10

Chives

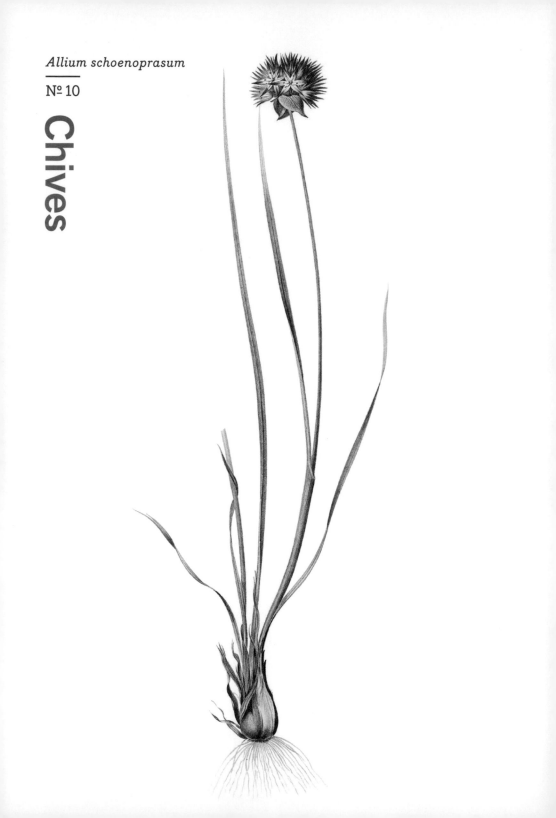

In the Victorian language of flowers, chives symbolize usefulness.

TO GROW

Chives thrive in well-drained soil with full sun, but light shade is also tolerable. They grow 12 to 18 inches in height and during the growing season continually regrow leaves, allowing for a continuous harvest. To harvest, take a selection of spears (leaves) in your hand (just what you need for dinner) and cut that section all the way to the ground. If you cut it mid-spear, that spear will turn into dead grass.

USAGE

Chives, along with tarragon, chervil, and parsley, are one of the four *fines herbes* of French cuisine. With their mild onion flavor, the diced green stalks (scapes) and unopened, immature flower buds are popular in potato salads, as a lentil soup garnish, and sprinkled on scrambled eggs or omelets. Although using the flowers is less common, some like to add them to salads, and they pair well with tomatoes. The flowers also make attractive additions to dried arrangements. Chives can be used in gardens to control pests (although note: bees are attracted to their nectar).

This mild member of the onion family is a perennial related to leeks, garlic, shallots, and scallions. The leaves and flowers are both edible, although the leaves are more common in recipes. The flowers are pale purple and grow in a cluster of ten to thirty, forming an attractive pompom atop the flower stalk. Chives grow widely throughout North America, Asia, and Europe, the only species of *Allium* native to both the Old and New Worlds. The species name is derived from the Greek words meaning "rush leek."

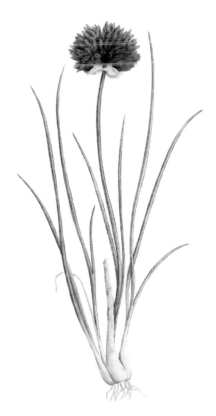

New Potatoes
with Chive Sour Cream

YIELD
—
Serves 6

These bite-size potatoes make delicious hors d'oeuvres, or a side for grilled or roasted fish.

1 8-ounce container sour cream
1 bunch chives (about ⅔ cup), minced
1 teaspoon salt
1 teaspoon white pepper
20 small red- or yellow-skinned new
       potatoes (approximately 2 pounds)
       Coarse salt for rolling

Preheat oven to 400 degrees.

Rinse the potatoes under cold water and roll in coarse salt.

Place on a baking sheet and roast until crinkly and soft, 15 to 20 minutes.

Remove from oven, cut each in half, and top with a dollop of sour cream mixture.

> **Note:** If you are grilling, these potatoes can be easily grilled for extra smoky flavor.

Cilantro

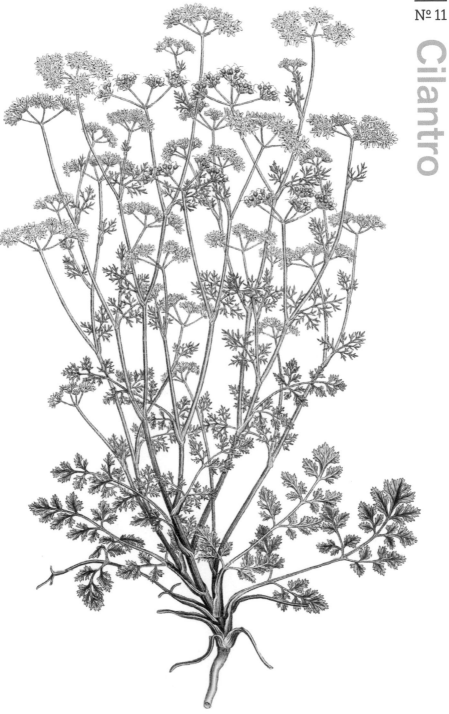

In the Victorian language of flowers, coriander stands for hidden worth.

TO GROW

Full sun and loamy, well-drained soil are optimal for growing cilantro, which will reach 2 feet. Make sure it stays adequately moist but do not overwater. Grow it near anise, but avoid fennel as a garden neighbor. In warmer months, cilantro will flower, a sign the plants are reaching the end of their harvesting days. After that, a bitter taste may result. When using fresh, be aware it keeps only a few days. A strong aroma and bright green color indicate the plant is fresh. The seed will be available to harvest shortly after flowering. Collect and dry the seeds and use within 6 months.

USAGE

Cilantro is traditional in Mexican cuisine and can often be found in salsa, chopped with tomatoes, onions, and jalapeños and accompanied by lime juice. In Asian cuisine cilantro is popular in chutney recipes and used lavishly as a garnish. Coriander seeds can be used to flavor chicken, rice, potatoes, and eggplant and also go well with ginger in carrot soup. Indian curries often include ground coriander, a popular spice in garam masala. The long-secret original recipe for Coca-Cola included coriander oil.

This hardy annual is also known as coriander or Chinese parsley. It is more closely related to carrots than parsley, despite its alternate name. The leaves have a strong, distinct, and pungent flavor that tends to inspire love or hate. All parts of the plant are edible. The leaves and stem are called cilantro and the seeds are referred to as coriander. The seed coriander is mentioned in Sanskrit texts and the Bible. Originating in Asia, Europe, and the Mediterranean, it was valued by the ancient Egyptians for a multitude of uses, both nutritional and medicinal. The dried seeds take on a lemony flavor with time.

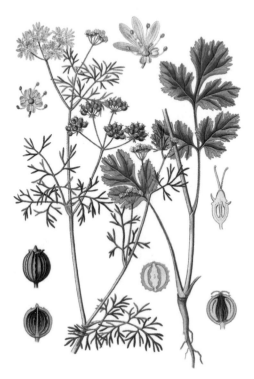

Green Guacamole

This spicy green dip is not for the faint of heart. It can serve as a salad as well as a dip because of the generous amount of cilantro included.

YIELD
_____

2 cups guacamole

2   ripe avocados (preferably Hass)
1   cup cilantro, stems trimmed, washed, and dried
4   scallions
1   fresh jalapeño
    Juice of 1 lime
    Salt to taste

Peel and chop the avocados and place in a bowl. Chop the scallions and cilantro and add to the bowl. Mince the jalapeño and add (scraping out the seeds if you prefer a milder dish). Add the lime juice and mix together until it reaches the consistency you like. Taste for salt.

Serve with chips of your choice.

Clary Sage

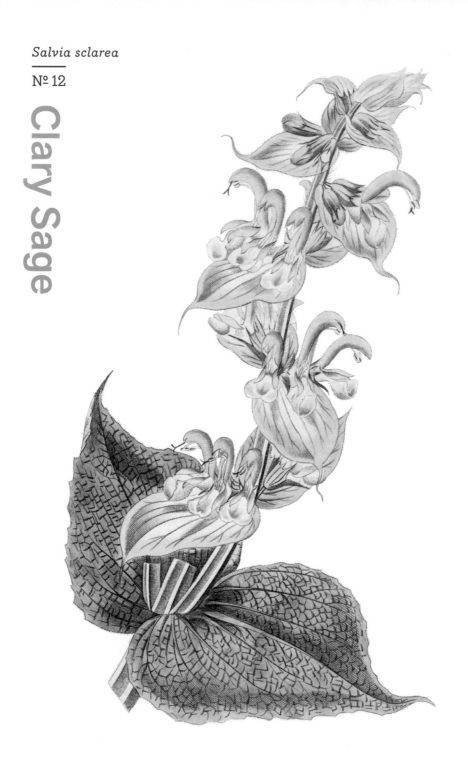

Clary sage was also called Oculos Christi or "Eye of Christ;" the Romans felt it increased spiritual as well as visual clarity.

TO GROW

Clary sage prefers full sun and moist environments, with well-drained soil. It can, however, tolerate dry conditions. It will grow 3 or 4 feet tall. Beginning in late spring, blue-purple flowers will appear. The leaves are best harvested for culinary purposes when young, as they grow bitter with age.

USAGE

Use as you would garden sage, adding either fresh or dried leaves to breads, stuffing, soups, omelets and jellies. A seventeenth-century recipe suggests dipping fresh leaves in a simple flour, egg, and milk batter, then frying them in butter. Clary sage makes an attractive garnish as well. The fragrant flowers, which are edible once the stems and greenery are removed, can be added to salads. Clary sage is used in vermouth and in muscatel-flavored wines. The naturally relaxing oil is used in various aromatherapies. With a fragrance similar to balsam, it is also popular in sachets, lotions, soaps, and detergents.

Clary sage, native to the Mediterranean and southern Europe, is also known as cleareye, orvale, eyebright, Europe sage, Muscatel sage, or simply clary. The Romans used the herb as an eyewash, referring to it as *sclarea*, from *claurus*, meaning clear. In the sixteenth century, German merchants had a different use—they found that by adding clary (along with elder flowers) to Rhine wine they could approximate a decent Muscatel; hence their name for it—*Muskateller Salbei*. The genus name is derived from the Latin *salvere*, to heal or save.

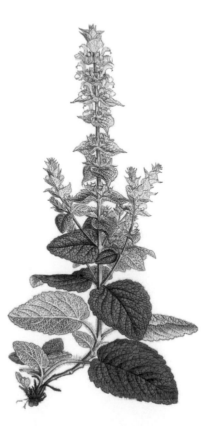

Zucchini with Clary Sage and Onion

A summer standard is enlivened by the woodsy flavor of clary sage leaves and the colorful blossoms as a garnish.

YIELD

———

Serves 6

4 medium zucchini, ends trimmed
1 large sweet onion, peeled and sliced crosswise
1 tablespoon olive oil
2 tablespoons butter
Juice of ½ lemon
3 teaspoons pure maple syrup
10 clary sage leaves, chopped
Salt and freshly ground pepper

Cut the zucchini lengthwise in half, then cut crosswise into ½-inch rounds. In a large skillet over medium heat, warm the olive oil and butter.

Add the onion and sauté until translucent. Add the zucchini and cook until all vegetables are slightly caramelized. Whisk the lemon juice, maple syrup, and chopped clary sage leaves in a bowl and pour over the sautéed vegetables. Salt and pepper to taste. Serve warm.

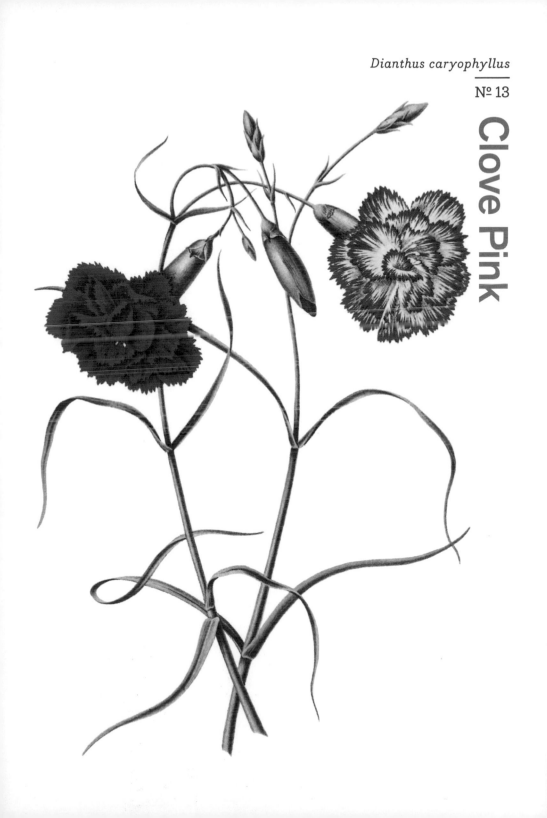

Clove Pink

In the language of flowers, clove pink refers to bonds of affection.

TO GROW
Grow in full sun. Soil should be moist and well drained. The hardy perennial will grow to 2 or 3 feet. It prefers alkaline but can tolerate a range of soils, as well as light frost, pollution, maritime conditions, and drought.

USAGE
Pick a bouquet to enjoy inside—they will last a long time as cut flowers— or add to potpourri mixes and pomanders. The flowers can be used as an edible garnish; just remove the bitter white heel before eating. Combine with oil, onion, parsley, marjoram, and Parmesan cheese for a unique pasta sauce. Clove pink can also be used in candied form and to flavor syrups, mulled wine, and liquors. The essential oil is used in perfumes. The lovely aroma will attract butterflies to the garden.

The carnations found in the florist shops today are descendants of clove pink, sometimes also called carnation. Other nicknames for clove pink include gillyflower, sweet William, wild carnation, and sometimes simply pinks. The aromatic flowers have a smell similar to cloves. With shorter stems than their more familiar counterparts, clove pinks are also distinguished by their more delicate flowers. The term "pink" is a reference to the leaf shape rather than the flower color, which can be white, red, lavender, or yellow in addition to pink. The word *pink* comes from Old English *pynken*. The plant's notched leaves may have reminded observers of the pattern left by pinking shears.

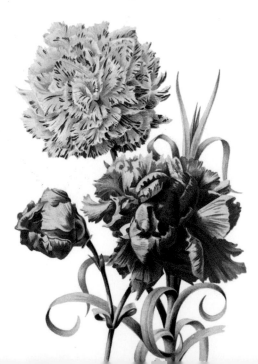

Clove Pink and Lavender Potpourri

A bowl of this delicately scented and hued potpourri refreshes any room in the house.

YIELD

Makes about 3 cups

- 4 cups clove pink flower heads
- 1 cup lavender flowers
- 5 drops lavender essential oil
- 10 cloves
- 3 cinnamon sticks, crushed

Preheat oven to 200 degrees.

Toss the clove pinks and lavender flowers in a bowl with 5 drops of the lavender oil. Spread on a baking sheet and sprinkle with the cloves and cinnamon.

Bake for up to 2 hours, until flowers feel crisp and dry. Any remaining moisture will result in moldy potpourri! Remove and divide between two pretty bowls.

Centaurea cyanus

№ 14

Cornflower

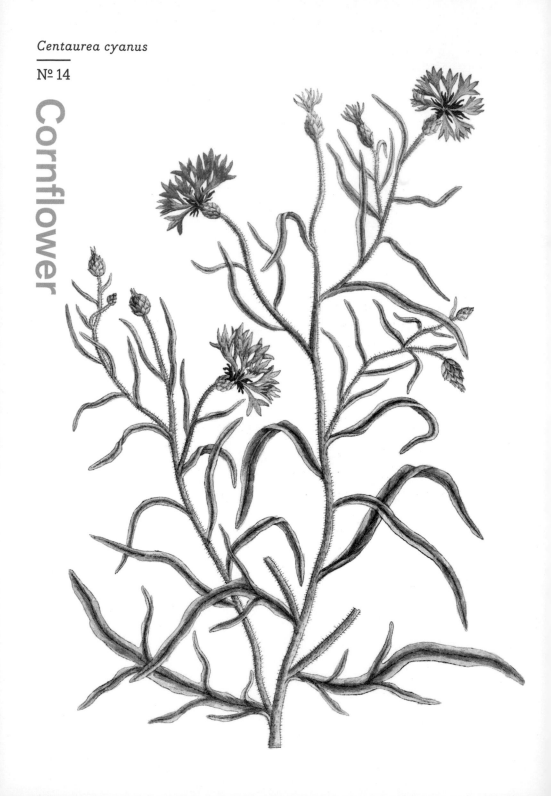

In the language of flowers, cornflower stands for delicacy and refinement.

TO GROW

This hardy annual prefers well-drained soil with moderate moisture and full sun to light shade. Several plantings can be made during a growing season.

USAGE

The edible petals have a slightly spicy, clove-like taste with a hint of sweetness. They add lovely color to salads and make spectacular candy lollipops. As with many edible flowers, the petals can be plucked and added to ice cubes, their brilliant color preserved for an elegant drink presentation.

Cornflower appears in some herbal tea blends and in Lady Grey tea. The long-lasting blooms are a hardy element in flower arrangements. The cornflower petals can also be boiled with alum, then strained to create a dye bath for blue pigment. Cornflower seeds attract a number of small seed-eating birds such as goldfinches. Bees and butterflies are also attracted to the blooms.

Cornflower, also called blue bottle or bachelor's button, is native to Europe but spread to North American and many other places, first introduced as an ornamental plant. The intense blue colors of the flowers are visible on long, solitary stalks rising above fields of corn or grains. The most valuable shade for blue sapphire gems is quite close to the blue of cornflowers. White, pink, and burgundy are now available as well. Historically cornflower grew in fields as a weed, but in its native habitat has become endangered by herbicides and industrial-scale agriculture. The genus name comes from the Greek *kentauros*, centaur. In Greek mythology, Chiron, a centaur and healer, applied cornflower blossoms to battle wounds.

The blue cornflower is Estonia's national flower. In France it is associated with the armistice of World War I and veterans, a parallel to the red poppies prized in the UK and the US. In Sweden the cornflower is a symbol of social liberalism.

Cornflower Sugar

Try mixing up a batch of cornflower sugar. The brilliant blue color of the flower will suffuse the sugar and make a dramatic dusting for dessert presentations.

YIELD

Makes ½ cup tinted sugar

2 cups cornflower petals
½ cup granulated sugar

Pluck the petals from two cups of cornflower heads. Grind them using a mortar and pestle into ½ cup of sugar, a few tablespoons at a time, until the sugar turns blue. Sprinkle the ground mixture onto a piece of parchment paper to dry overnight or place in the oven on low heat (120 degrees) for 2 hours. Store in an airtight container.

Dandelion

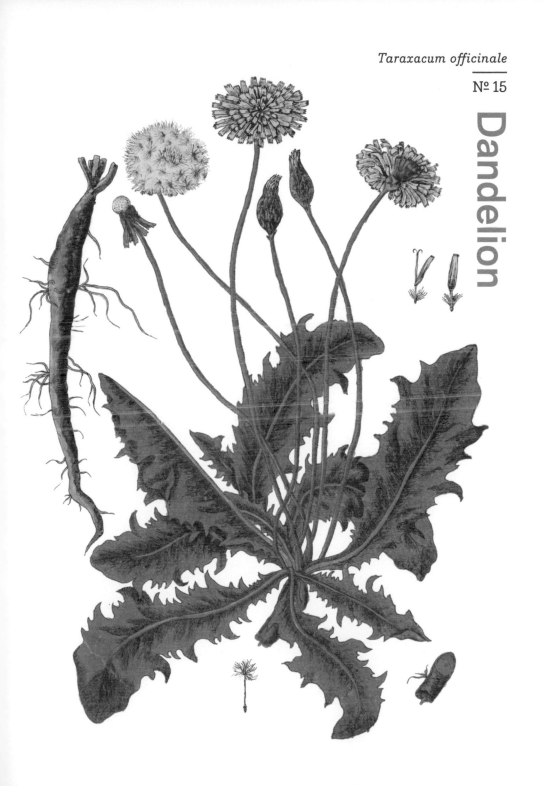

Dandelions represent cheerfulness and resilience. They're also associated with wish fulfillment.

TO GROW

Dandelions don't need any help growing. They are self-pollinating, and have a taproot that extends deep into the soil and can regrow the plant. Harvest greens before flowering for optimum taste.

USAGE

The whole dandelion is edible. A nutritious plant, it is high in vitamins A and K as well as iron. Blanch the leaves and sauté with garlic and oil, plus a squeeze of lemon when serving. Flowers are enjoyed in their yellow form before they turn to seed heads. They can be infused to flavor honey, syrup, vinegar, and wine. A coffee alternative can be produced by roasting and grinding the roots. Make flowers into fritters with a batter of flour, eggs, and milk. The British drink called dandelion and burdock is made with the ubiquitous herb, which is also one of the ingredients in traditional root beer. Dandelions are important source of nectar for range of pollinators.

Dandelions are also known as fairy clocks, lion's teeth, Irish daisy, fortune teller, heart fever grass, burning fire, timeteller, burning fire, and piss-a-bed. In the same family as chamomile, dandelions likely originated in Eurasia roughly 30 million years ago. The ancient Chinese valued the hardy perennial for its medicinal properties. Arabic physicians in the eleventh century or possibly earlier used dandelions for a liver treatment. Colonists, including the Mayflower pilgrims, likely introduced the once-cherished herb to American landscapes. The Pillager Ojibwas and Mohegans made a wellness tea by boiling the dandelions in water. Having spread worldwide in recent decades, they have become one of the most despised lawn-invading weeds.

The English name dandelion is adapted from the French *dent de lion*, meaning lion's tooth, a reference to the jagged leaves. Many children believe blowing on the white seed head will make their wish come true. It will certainly aid in seed dispersal.

Dandelion Fritters

These crunchy, shaggy bites are an irresistible way to enjoy the sunny heads of dandelion flowers.

YIELD

———

Makes 20 fritters

½   cup all-purpose flour
1   scant teaspoon baking powder
1   teaspoon salt
½   tablespoon nutritional yeast
1   large egg
¾   cup milk
1   teaspoon dried thyme
¼   cup chopped chives or scallions (optional)
1   teaspoon vegetable oil, plus oil for frying
1   cup dandelion flowers (about 20 heads), washed and dried

Recipe continues on next page

In a bowl, mix flour, baking powder, salt, and nutritional yeast. In a separate bowl, beat the egg and milk, then stir into the dry ingredients. Add the thyme, then the chives or scallions if using.

Heat the oil in a deep frying pan until a crumb sizzles when dropped in. Dip each flower head into the batter and coat well. Fry the flowers in batches. Start with the petal side down and flip when light brown, making sure both sides are crisp.

Serve with plain yogurt on the side.

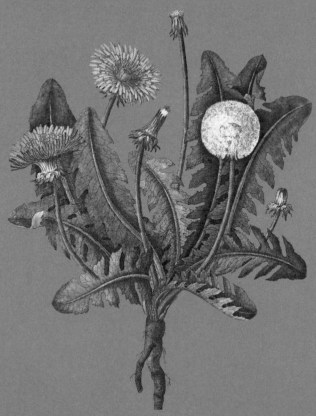

Dill

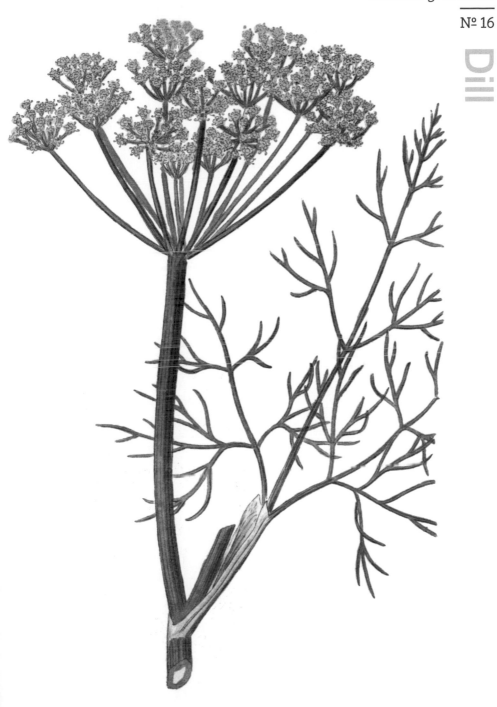

In the language of flowers, dill stands for power against evil.

TO GROW
Grow in full sun in a spot protected from strong wind, keeping soil moist but well drained. Will reach 2 feet or sometimes as high as 4 and spreads easily. Warm weather will produce flowering or "bolting," at which point the leaves begin to taste bitter. Avoid planting near carrots, which impede its growth. Fennel, dill, and carrot are members of the same family and can easily cross-pollinate, which can adversely effect flavor and growth. The dill plant will bring butterflies and bees to the garden. Harvest before flowers bloom and in the early part of the day. Use fresh just after harvesting, as it wilts quickly.

USAGE
Cucumber and potato salads are enhanced by dill. Try adding it to cold cucumber and yogurt soups or roasted carrots. Dill goes well on top of fried or scrambled eggs, ideally added just before serving for the freshest flavor. In the popular Greek stuffed grape leaves, dolmadakia, the filling features dillweed, rice, and mint. Dill vinegar can be made from the seeds.

An aromatic annual in the same family as celery and parsley, dill is native to the Mediterranean and western Asia. The name comes from Norse *dylla*, to soothe. Popular in a range of European cuisines, dill is referred to in texts as far back as ancient Egypt and was grown by the Babylonians. The ancient Romans and Greeks made use of dill seeds in healing treatments. The whole plant is edible. With a flavor likened to sweet grass and sometimes licorice, it has seeds with a taste similar to fennel or caraway. The herb dill or dillweed comes from the delicate green leaves. The spice dill refers to the seeds, used to make dill pickles, for example.

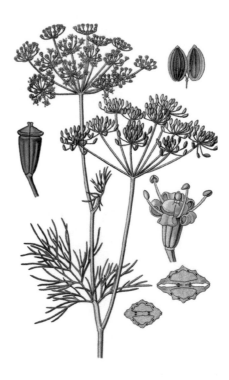

Greek Romaine and Dill Salad

This addictive salad takes about 5 minutes to make and accompanies grilled fish and chicken particularly well.

YIELD

Serves 6

1	large head romaine lettuce, washed and spun dry
5	scallions, washed and trimmed
1	cup dill, washed and spun dry
3	tablespoons olive oil
1	tablespoon red wine vinegar
1	cup crumbled feta cheese
	Salt and freshly ground pepper to taste

Stack the lettuce leaves in a pile and cut crosswise into thin strips. Place in a large salad bowl. Chop the scallions crosswise into rounds, including the green stalks, and add to the bowl. Snip the dill into the bowl with scissors down to 1 inch from the end of the stem. Drizzle the olive oil and vinegar over all. Add the feta and toss well. Add salt and pepper to taste.

Fennel

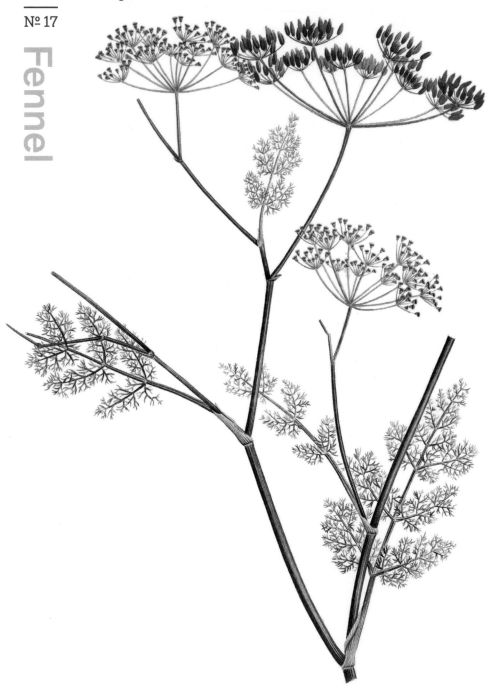

In the Victorian language of flowers, fennel means worthy of praise.

TO GROW

Dry soils near the ocean or along riverbanks provide the best conditions for growing the fennel herb, which grows 3 to 5 feet tall. In late summer, groups of yellow flowers will appear. The shorter vegetable fennel maxes at approximately 2 feet and has darker foliage. The "bulb" is the main prize: It can be harvested when it reaches tennis ball size and eaten raw or cooked. Store in a cool location for a few weeks. Either type of fennel can be produced from seed in full sun and soil rich with organic matter. Avoid planting near dill, coriander, wormwood, beans, tomatoes, caraway, and cabbage.

USAGE

Fish dishes, as well as soups and stews, are enhanced by fennel, and the seed is a common flavoring for sausage. Try the bulbs sautéed. They are lovely roasted with salt and olive oil and make a delightful combination served raw with pears and Parmesan cheese. A range of foods from meats to ice cream to baked goods, liquors, and toothpaste are prepared with fennel oil or seeds, and the essential oil enhances perfumes and cosmetics. The seeds are said to freshen breath and reduce hunger. They're popular in India served directly after a meal.

Fennel is native to the Mediterranean and cultivated worldwide. Belonging to the same family as carrots and parsley, it is—along with anise—a main ingredient in the liquor absinthe. The United States gets most of its commercial fennel seed from Egypt. Another type of fennel, Florence fennel or Finocchio, is treated like a vegetable. Both the herb and vegetable forms have a flavor that resembles licorice.

Fennel features prominently in the Greek myth of humans acquiring the gift of fire. Prometheus, according to the Greek myth, stole fire from the gods and found a convenient hiding place: a stalk of fennel with a hollow inside. The legendary Battle of Marathon took place on a field full of fennel, hence the Greek word for fennel— *marathon*. The famed messenger who ran 150 miles in two days' time was said to be holding a stalk of fennel as he ran to keep him going.

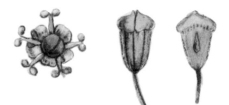

Cod Roasted on a Bed of Fennel

Precooking the fennel and onions makes a tender bed for the cod. If you have leftovers (unlikely), this is delicious cold the day after, sauced with lemon and mayonnaise. Save the fennel fronds for a garnish.

2	fennel bulbs (the thick base of the stalk), stalks cut off, bulbs halved lengthwise, and sliced thinly into ¼-inch strips
1	sweet onion, halved and sliced into ¼-inch strips
¼	cup olive oil
1½	pounds cod
1	tablespoon Dijon mustard
¼	cup dry white wine or vermouth
¼	cup breadcrumbs
	Salt and freshly ground pepper

Preheat oven to 400 degrees.

Toss the fennel and onion slices with olive oil. Spread them across the bottom of an 8 × 11- inch baking pan and roast until translucent and tender, about 20 minutes.

Remove from the oven and toss with a fork. Arrange the cod over the cooked vegetables.

Spread the mustard over the cod, then drizzle with wine or vermouth. Sprinkle breadcrumbs over all, then salt and pepper lightly. Return to oven and roast until the cod is cooked through (it will flake easily when poked). Check it after 10 minutes so it doesn't dry out.

Fenugreek

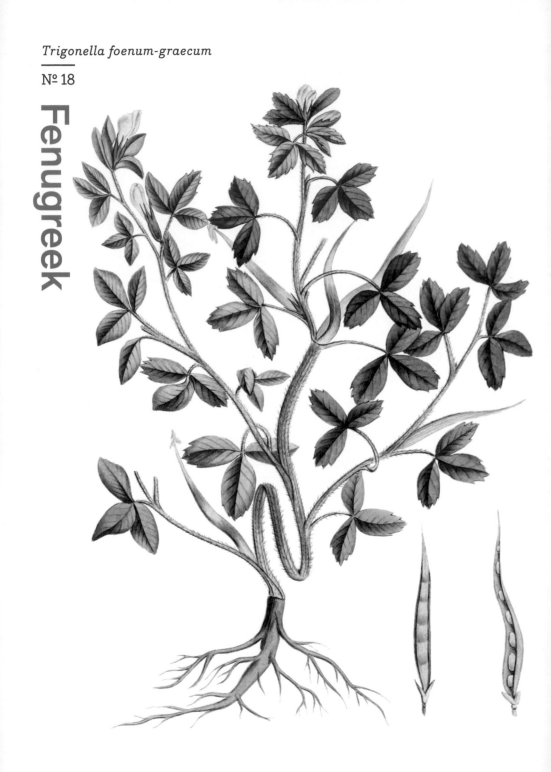

Emperor Charlemagne was a champion of fenugreek, which grew in his imperial gardens.

This clover-like annual is part of the bean family, known for a fragrance similar to maple syrup. It is believed that fenugreek was first cultivated in the Middle East. Tutankhamun's tomb was found to contain fenugreek seeds, and the Romans used it to flavor wine. The name comes from the Latin *faenum graecum,* which translates to Greek hay. India is the biggest producer of the herb, and the seeds and leaves are popular flavors on the Indian subcontinent. Fenugreek has spread worldwide.

TO GROW

Fenugreek does well in full sun but can tolerate a bit of shade in the afternoons. Keep the soil moist and well drained. In summer, white or yellow flowers appear. The pods contain the seeds—10 to 20 each—that are dried to produce the spice known commercially as fenugreek.

USAGE

In India, pickles, spice mixes, and curries commonly include fenugreek. Flatbread sprinkled with fenugreek seeds is a popular dish in Egypt, where the seeds are also boiled into a beverage. In Israel, New Year's celebrations feature a relish using fenugreek. The leaves can be incorporated into salads and eaten as a vegetable. The smell is like maple syrup, which makes fenugreek a useful ingredient for creating imitation maple flavor.

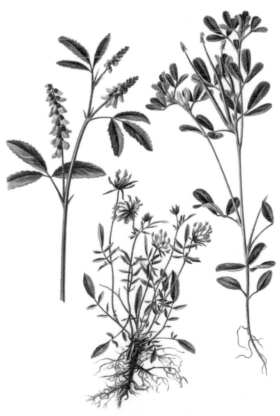

Helba (Egyptian Tea)

This traditional Egyptian tea has a deep nutty flavor. Soaking the seeds overnight in water makes them milder and easier to pulverize.

YIELD
___

Serves 2

2 teaspoons fenugreek seeds
  Water

Soak the fenugreek seeds in a glass of water overnight. Strain and roughly crush the seeds in a mortar and pestle. Put them in a small saucepan with 2 cups cold water and heat until boiling. Reduce heat and simmer for 3 to 5 minutes. Remove from heat and steep for 8 to 10 minutes. Strain liquid into 2 mugs. To make more sweet or tart, add a teaspoon of sugar or lemon juice. A sprinkle of cinnamon, while not traditional, complements the tea's maple flavor.

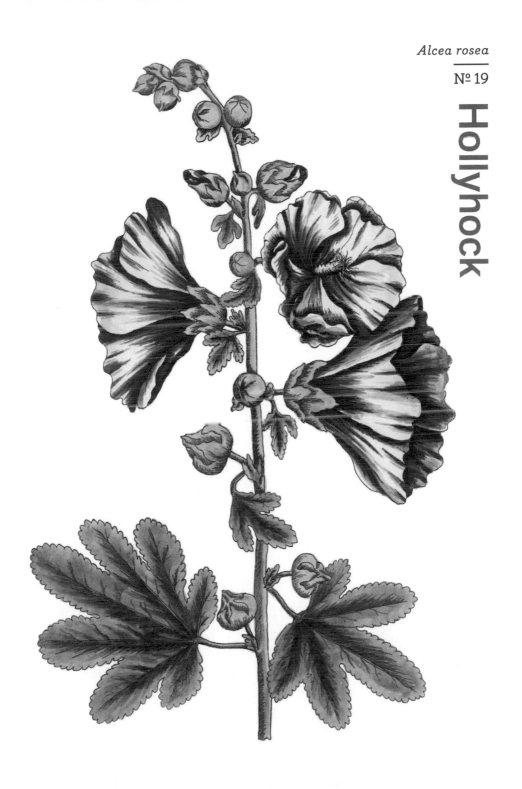

Alcea rosea

№ 19

Hollyhock

In the Victorian language of flowers, the hollyhock symbolizes both ambition and fertility.

TO GROW

Hollyhocks grow easily from seed. They prefer full sun, are drought resistant (only needing watering when extremely dry), and do well in poor soils. Hollyhocks do not require support initially, but they should be staked once they top 3 feet and are covered in large blossoms. They will attract butterflies and hummingbirds to the garden. Hollyhock roots are tougher than those of its cousin the marsh mallow.

USAGE

Petals are nontoxic and, while not flavorful, they make a pretty garnish for desserts. Some use them to repair split ends in hair or infuse into soap. The petals of the dark purple variety, *Alcea rosea 'Nigra',* can be used to dye wool.

This popular old-fashioned perennial is a member of the Malvaceae family. Native to Europe and Asia. Its blooms range in color from red to purple, pink, white, and yellow. Reaching up to 8 feet in height, hollyhock is an essential feature of the classic cottage garden. In a book commissioned by Anne of Brittany, Queen of France, hollyhocks are called *roses d'oustremer,* meaning roses from overseas.

In Japan, an annual hollyhock festival called Aoi Matsuri has been celebrated in May for hundreds of years.

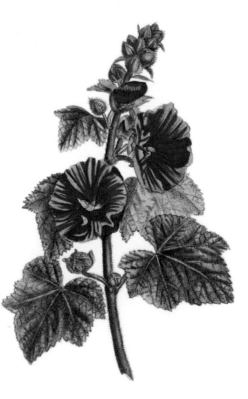

Hollyhock Dolls

These cheerful dolls make a great garden activity and natural decoration. If you have different hollyhocks in bloom, you can have a doll party! Pick a small unopened flower bud and carefully peel away the green underside. This will become the head of the doll. Then pick a fully opened flower and turn it upside-down to become the doll's ruffled skirt. Attach the head to the flower bottom using a toothpick. Additional toothpicks can be used for the arms. They look sweet arranged around a birthday cake or as a table arrangement for an outdoor dinner.

Arrubium vulgare

№ 20

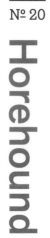

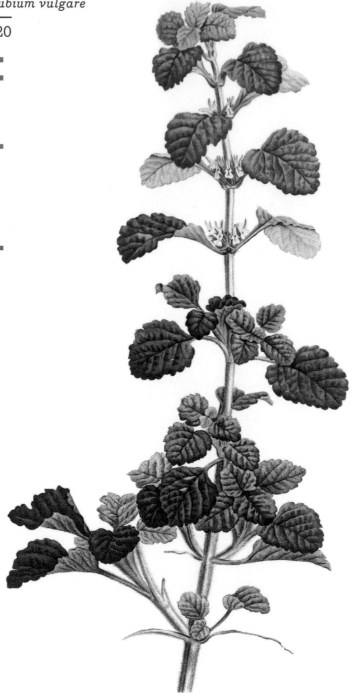

In the language of flowers, horehound stands for health.

TO GROW
Horehound is easy to grow, even in poor soil with little water, and can reach 3 feet in height. Although it will not have blossoms—small, whitish flowers—until its second year, it can grow rapidly and will need to be watched so it does not take over too much space.

USAGE
A primary ingredient in Ricola, the cough drop from the Swiss Alps, horehound is valued as a cough suppressant and for clearing congestion. It is also enjoyed in candy form as horehound drops, with a flavor likened to menthol, root beer, and licorice. Leaves and flowers can be added to soups and salads and the herb can be made into ale and tea.

White horehound or common horehound, also called eye of the star, is a hardy, aromatic perennial in the mint family. The flowering plant is native to the Mediterranean, North Africa, and parts of Asia. Greek physician Galen wrote about horehound in the first century AD.

Egyptian priests called it seed of Horus, and its common name may have derived from this moniker. A possible origin of the Latin name is the Hebrew word *marrob* (a bitter juice); it's possible that horehound was one of the "bitter herbs" eaten at Passover. Imported into Australia and New Zealand in the 1800s, horehound has developed into an invasive weed. The scent attracts bees, but the fragrance resembling thyme lasts only until the flowers dry.

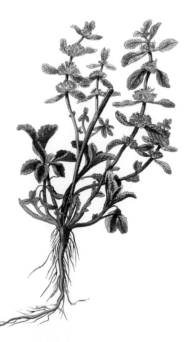

Rock and Rye Cocktail

Rock and Rye goes back a long way in America; it may have started as a way to disguise the taste of cheap alcohol, and had a long run as a homemade cold remedy—which it most definitely is not. It is, however, quite tasty, and the recipe can be tweaked to suit individual preferences.

YIELD

Makes 1 bottle (750 ml; 26 ounces) flavored whiskey

- **1** bottle (750 ml or 26 ounces) rye whiskey
- **8** ounces rock candy, about a 6-inch string
- **1** maraschino cherry (preferably Luxardo) plus 1 tablespoon of the syrup
- **3** whole cloves
- **1** whole star anise
- **1** stick cinnamon
- **1** sprig horehound or 1 teaspoon dried horehound
- **1** orange, sliced thin
- **1** lemon, sliced thin

Stir ingredients together in a glass quart jar with a lid. Let steep at room temperature for at least 2 days or up to 1 month. Strain through a coffee filter into a clean bottle and store in a cool, dark location.

Lavender

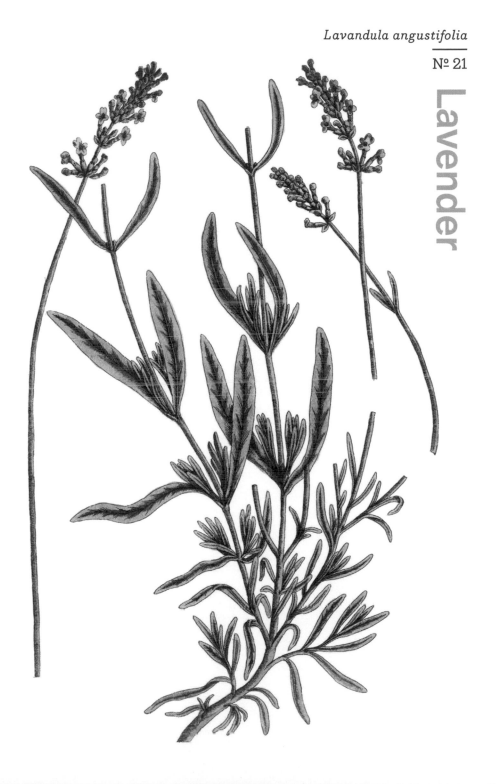

In the Victorian language of flowers, lavender stands for distrust.

Native to the Mediterranean, common lavender is a fragrant perennial also called English lavender, narrow-leaved lavender, or just lavender. A member of the mint family, it is beloved for its scent and purplish flowers, one of some 47 species of *Lanvandula*.

TO GROW

Lavender likes full sun and well drained soil and will reach up to 3 feet. Begin with cuttings. Once it has taken root, it will need only a small amount of water. They are frequently enjoyed as indoor container plants. Harvest early in the day after dew has dried and hang upside down to dry.

The ancient Romans used lavender to keep insects away and as a balm for bites. The genus names may have come from the Latin *lavare*, to wash, perhaps related to the Roman practice of using lavender in washing. In the Middle Ages, it was a strewing herb to freshen air inside.

USAGE

Lavender is treasured for its scent, although also used as a garnish or flavoring. Lavender flavoring can be found in ice cream, jams, lemon bars, cookies, cakes, tarts, salad dressings, cocktails, lemonades, spritzers, teas and even lattes. Tremendously popular for potpourri, sachets, and dream pillows, lavender is calming and believed by many to be sleep inducing. Used in meditation, aromatherapy, perfumes, soaps, skin lotions, shampoos and conditioners. Also enjoyed in fresh bouquets. Attracts bees to the garden and, inside the closet, repels moths.

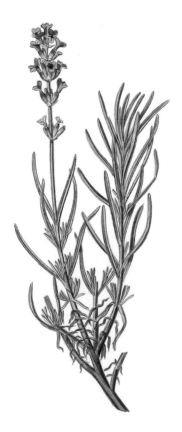

Lavender Lemonade

Steep fragrant lavender and add to classic lemonade for a refreshingly different twist on an old favorite.

YIELD
—
Makes 6 servings

- ¼ cup dried lavender
- 2 cups boiling water
- ¾ cup white sugar
  Juice of 8 lemons
- 5 cups cold water, or as needed
- ¼ cup grape juice (optional)

Put the lavender in a bowl and pour the boiling water over it. Allow to steep for about 10 minutes, then strain out the lavender and discard. Mix the sugar into the hot lavender water, then pour into a pitcher filled with ice.

Stir in the lemon juice and fill the pitcher to the brim. Top off the pitcher with cold water and stir. Adjust to taste with additional sugar or lemon juice. Adding ¼ cup of grape juice will give the lemonade a lavender tint!

Melissa officinalis

Nº 22

Lemon Balm

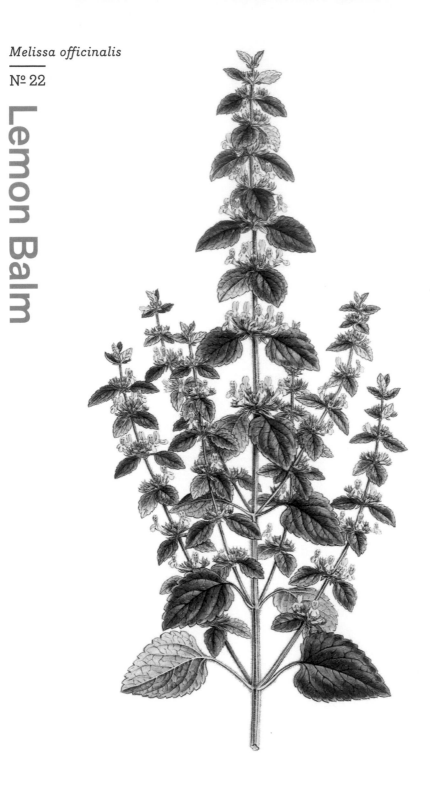

In the language of flowers, lemon balm represents sympathy.

TO GROW

Reaching 5 feet, lemon balm grows easily in groups. Sunny, moist, well-drained areas serve it best, but lemon balm is adaptive and will tolerate a range of conditions. Plant with angelica and nasturtiums, but just be sure to give it a little distance from these other plants. Broccoli, cauliflower, and other cabbage family plants also make good neighbors. Planting near fruit trees will aid pollination by bringing honeybees to the area. If it becomes invasive, simply snip off the flower heads, thereby removing the seed. Harvest before flowering, when the lemon aroma is said to be at its peak. Fresh leaves are more flavorful than dried.

USAGE

The lemony-flavored leaves are used in teas and as a flavoring in ice cream, candies, baked goods, cheesecakes, fruit cups, marinades, alcoholic beverages, and toothpaste. Leaves can liven up fruit juices and sodas. Iced tea can be enhanced with a small amount of lemon balm distillate. Leaves make an aromatic garnish. The herb can also be used in dips and salads and to season fish dishes. The liqueurs Benedictine and Chartreuse both contain lemon balm. For a cozy

A perennial plant in the mint family, lemon balm is also called balm mint, and sometimes bee balm but not to be confused with another plant—*Monarda didyma*—also called bee balm. Bees are attracted to the nectar inside the small white flowers produced in summer. The genus name, *Melissa* (Greek for honeybee), pays tribute to this quality. Native to southern Europe, the Mediterranean, Central Asia, and Iran, lemon balm was introduced to North America when early colonists used it as a less-expensive substitute for lemons. Thomas Jefferson's garden at Monticello is said to have included the herb. Its recorded history goes much further back, however. Ancient Greek herbalist Theophrastus called the plant honey leaf in 300 BC, and in the Middle Ages it was employed in Europe as a strewing herb, scattered on floors to freshen up the inside air.

nighttime drink, steep leaves in hot milk for 5 minutes, strain out the leaves, and add 1 teaspoon maple syrup. It will also add a delicate flavor to oatmeal; again, strain after steeping.

Add fresh to flower arrangements and dried to potpourri and sleep pillows. The oil is used in perfumes and as a wood polish.

Lemon Balm Vinaigrette

This is delicious on fennel salads or as a dip for artichokes.

YIELD
———
Makes 1 cup vinaigrette

2 scallions with their green stalks, minced

2 tablespoons lemon balm, minced

½ teaspoon lemon zest

1 tablespoon fresh lemon juice

4 tablespoons rice wine vinegar

1 teaspoon Dijon mustard

⅓ cup olive oil

Salt and freshly ground pepper to taste

Mix together the scallions, lemon balm, zest and juice of the lemon, and mustard, then whisk in the oil. Add a pinch of salt and pepper. Whisk again before serving. It will last in the refrigerator for about a week.

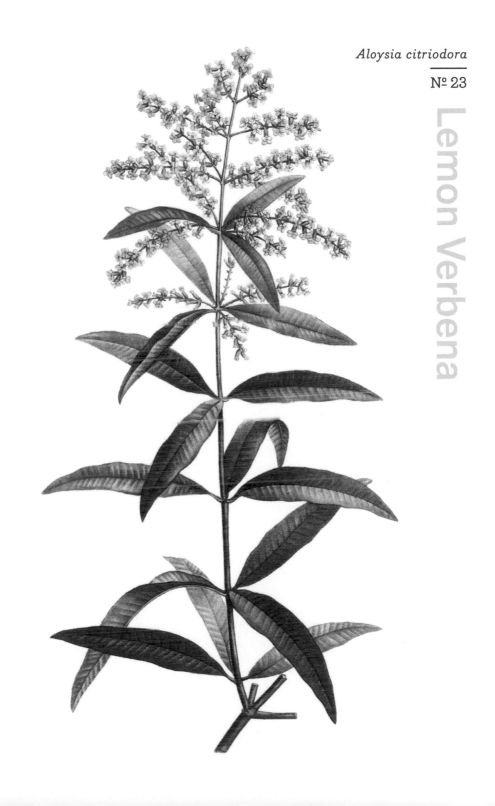

Aloysia citriodora

N̲º̲ 23

Lemon Verbena

In the language of flowers, lemon verbena symbolizes sensitivity.

TO GROW

Grow in full sun, watering regularly and making sure soil is well drained. Easy to grow from cuttings. Does well planted along paths. Growing outside in warm climates is ideal. It may reach 8 feet or even higher. In containers, lemon verbena will likely grow to only 3 feet or less.

USAGE

Try it in any recipe as a lemon substitute. Some use for a lemongrass substitute as well. Complements chicken and fish dishes. Lovely mixed into butter. Found in teas, martinis, dressings, syrups, custards, ice cream, puddings, and various baked goods. Try on fruit desserts and yogurt parfaits. Mince leaves first and add toward the end of the preparation process. Can also be used to make lemon-flavored sugar. The robust fragrance of dried lemon verbena makes it popular for sachets and potpourri. It's often found in cleaning products, perfumes, soaps, lotions, and other skin care products.

Native to South America, lemon verbena is also called lemon beebrush, vergain, or herb louisa. In taste and smell, it resembles lemon. The species name, *citriodora*, is Latin for lemon scented. The woody shrub has long been valued as a calming tea. Spanish colonizers brought the plant to Europe in the seventeenth century. The genus name, a variant of Louisa, is said to come from Maria Louisa of Parma, a Spanish princess. The Victorians became quite fond of the tender perennial, sewing it into clothing, gathering it in handkerchiefs, and adding it to nosegays. It makes an appearance in both *Gone with the Wind* and *Little House on the Prairie*.

Lemon Verbena Limoncello Granita

Topped with raspberries, this makes a stunning summer dessert.

YIELD
___

Makes 1 quart; serves 4

1   cup sugar
1   teaspoon finely chopped lemon verbena leaves
1   cup fresh lemon juice (about 6 lemons)
¼   cup limoncello

Combine ½ cup water and the sugar in a saucepan over medium heat. Heat, stirring frequently, until the sugar is dissolved. Remove from heat and stir in 2 cups of water and the lemon verbena. Refrigerate the mixture until cold, about 2 hours. Stir the lemon juice and limoncello into the sugar mixture. Freeze in a covered container until solid. Unmold into a blender and pulse, pushing down the sides until the mixture is grainy but not mushy. Garnish with more finely chopped leaves or lemon zest, if desired.

Lovage

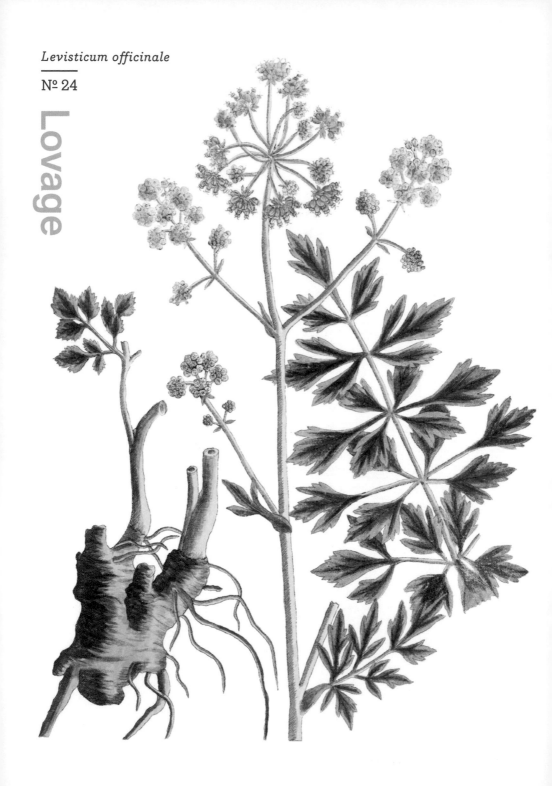

In the secret language of flowers, lovage symbolizes strength.

This tall perennial, also known as false celery, or Maggie Herb in Germany and Holland, resembles celery and parsley in taste. Lovage originated in Persia and became popular in the Mediterranean, where ancient Greeks and Romans valued it to flavor food and for its healing properties. The roots can be eaten as a vegetable and the seeds used as a spice. The bright yellow flowers are marvelously fragrant in midsummer. *Ligusticum scotium*, also known as Scottish lovage or Scottish licorice root, is a less common relative of *Levisticum officinale* that looks similar but has a bolder flavor.

TO GROW

Lovage is hardy and prefers moist soil but can manage in partial shade and may grow to 6 feet. Keeping the soil moist will prevent it from turning to seed too early in hot and dry conditions, and organic matter will help it grow. Lovage needs plenty of space to spread out. Hot and dry conditions encourage it to run to seed, so it is best if the roots are kept damp by watering in dry weather. Keep the soil moist to the touch at all times, but not wet. If the soil dries out, the leaves tend to get bitter. Add an inch or two of mulch to help retain water. If the plant bolts and starts to develop a flower stalk, cut it off unless you want the plant to flower and set seed. After bolting, the leaves can be unpleasantly bitter. The leaves do not retain much flavor when dried.

USAGE

Lovage can be substituted in any recipe that calls for celery. Egg salads, potato salads, and pasta salads are all perked up with the addition of lovage. The leaves will enhance salads and add a nice flavor to soups, and the roots can be treated like celeriac and eaten as a vegetable. The seeds, similar to fennel, can be used as a spice. In Romania lovage is popular for pickling cabbage and cucumbers and for making broths.

Lovage Tuna Salad

Lovage takes the place of celery in this sprightly version of the classic tuna salad.

YIELD

Serves 4

2	cans tuna, packed in oil
3	tablespoons mayonnaise
1	teaspoon rice wine vinegar
1	teaspoon Dijon mustard
	Dash Worcestershire sauce
1	tablespoon capers, drained
2	scallions, chopped with greens
½	cup fresh lovage leaves, finely chopped
1	cup cherry tomatoes, halved
2	cups mixed greens

Drain the tuna, place in a medium-size bowl, and flake with a fork. Add all ingredients except the tomatoes and greens and mix thoroughly. Spread mixed greens on a platter, spoon the tuna mixture over, and scatter cherry tomatoes on top.

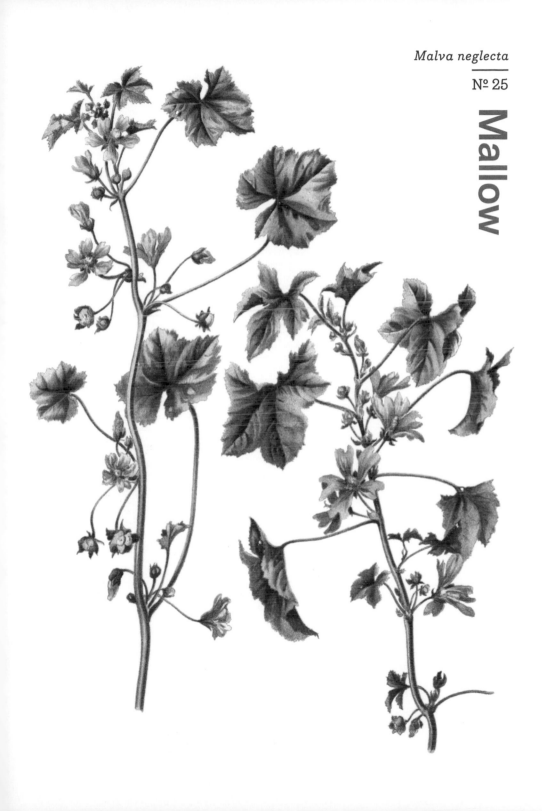

The popular treat called marshmallow was originally made from sap extracted from roots of the marsh-growing mallow.

TO GROW

Mallow can grow up to 2 feet in height in moist areas and will flower starting in late spring, producing seedpods at the start of summer. The round seedpods, called cheeseheads, come after flowering. Harvest leaves in the spring when they're green.

USAGE

The fruiting heads look like a wheel of cheese. Try them raw, but don't expect a cheese-like flavor, as mallow has very little flavor of its own, assuming instead the flavor of companion ingredients. It's a nutritious plant, rich in calcium, magnesium, potassium, and vitamins A, B, and C. Young leaves are bursting with vitamin A.

Try sautéing mallow with oil, onion, and garlic as you would spinach or Swiss chard or employing as a thickener in soups. Can be added to salads, veggie patties, pastas, and quiches. In China, mallow roots are used for broths. Frying slices of the roots in oil makes wonderful mallow chips; for a healthier version, bake them. The pickled fruits can be substituted for capers.

Belonging to the same plant family as cotton and hibiscus, mallow is also known as buttonweed, cheeseweed, and common or dwarf mallow. *Malva*, its genus name, comes from the Greek word for soft: *malakos*. Native to Asia and Europe, the color of its flowers varies from white to mauve or pink to yellow to blue to lavender. Its leaves are similar to those on geranium leaves.

The Bible references mallow, and its common name means bread in both Arabic and Hebrew. An important source of sustenance during famine, all members of the family Malvaceae except the cotton plant (*Gossypium hirsutum*) are said to be edible.

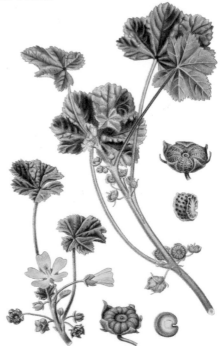

Mallow Miso Soup

Mallow behaves a lot like seaweed in a miso soup. Simply replace the seaweed with dried mallow leaves.

YIELD
———
Serves 4

6 cups vegetable broth
¾ cup dried mallow leaves
4 tablespoons white miso
4 scallions, minced
½ pound soft tofu, drained and cut into ½-inch cubes

Heat the vegetable broth in a deep saucepan until just boiling. Turn off heat and add mallow leaves to soften. Transfer ½ cup of hot broth to a bowl and whisk in the miso. When mallow leaves are tender, whisk in the miso-vegetable broth. Reheat until simmering and remove from heat. Scatter in the scallions and serve.

Origanum majorana

№ 26

Marjoram

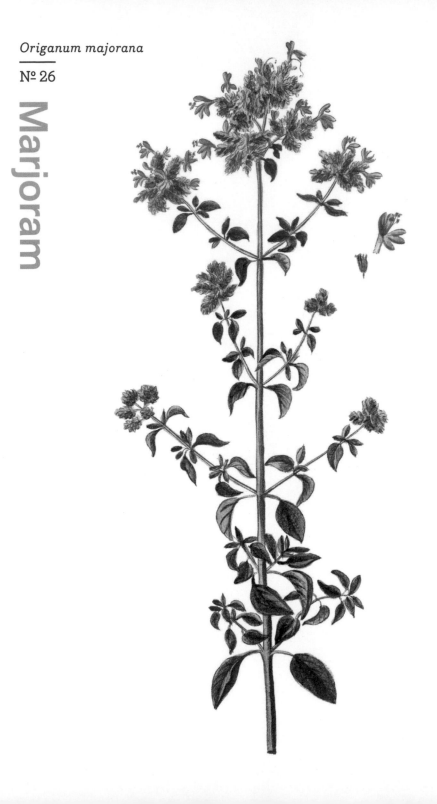

In the language of flowers, marjoram represents joy and happiness.

TO GROW

Grows best indoors in cooler climates. Sweet marjoram is simple to cultivate and doesn't weaken easily. It will sprout rapidly and can endure dry soil. Pick sweet marjoram directly after blossoms appear and enjoy fresh or dried. All but the roots are edible.

USAGE

Most suitable for savory foods, marjoram is often found in the French *herbes de Provence* mixture and also in the Middle Eastern spice mix *za'atar*. Pairing well with lemon and a popular seasoning for chicken, the sweet-smelling spice is also used to season egg dishes, sauces, soups, and stews. Marjoram tea is said to help with digestion. The aroma lasts well when dry, making it a favorite for herb-based potpourri.

This tender perennial herb is native to Turkey, Cyprus, Arabia, and the eastern Mediterranean region. A member of the mint family, it is closely related to oregano, but with a milder flavor; in fact, some countries consider the cousin herbs to be the same. However, there is only one true marjoram in the genus *Origanum*, which contains approximately forty species altogether.

Before sporting its white or pink flowers, the ancient herb, called the "herb of grace" by Shakespeare, grows buds that resemble knots, the origin of a common alternate name: knotted marjoram. Marjoram symbolized happiness to Greeks and Romans; the word comes from the Greek meaning joy of the mountain, and the fragrance was associated with the goddess Aphrodite. It was once a tradition for newlyweds to wear marjoram twined into garlands. Americans did not become familiar with marjoram until the mid-1900s.

White Bean Soup with Pastina and Marjoram Pistou

This simple soup is delicious poured over a slice of toasted bread rubbed with garlic and finished with olive oil.

YIELD

Serves 4

4	cups chicken broth
1½	cups cooked cannellini beans
1	cup orzo or pastina
¼	cup fresh minced marjoram
4	tablespoons grated Parmesan cheese
½	teaspoon salt
2 to 3	tablespoons olive oil
4	slices garlic-rubbed toast

Put the broth in a large saucepan and bring to a boil. Add the beans, then stir in the pasta and cook until al dente, about 10 minutes.

In a mortar and pestle, mash the marjoram and Parmesan with olive oil until you have a thick paste. Season with salt.

Place a slice of garlic-rubbed toast at the bottom of 4 soup bowls. Pour soup over each and swirl in a spoonful of pistou before serving.

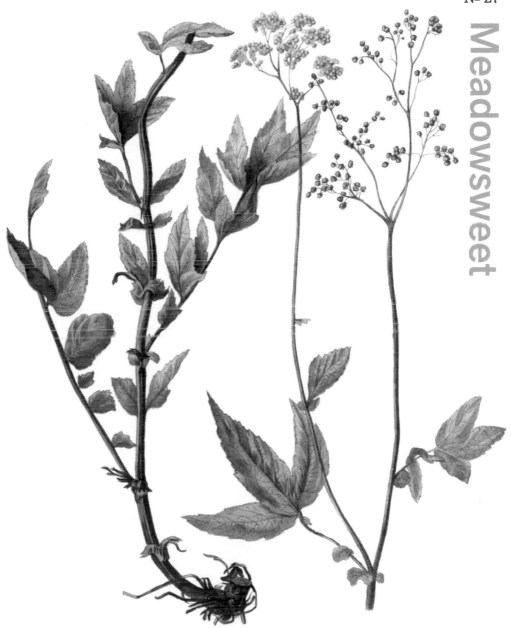

Meadowsweet

In the language of flowers, meadowsweet is said to stand for uselessness.

TO GROW

Choose partial shade and keep the soil moist. The plant will reach between 3 to 6 feet, at which point it will soar above surrounding plants—the queen of the meadow. Pick the plant and harvest leaves and flowers after flowering.

USAGE

Sorbets and fruit salads will be livened up with the addition of fresh meadowsweet leaves. Although leaves act as sweeteners, the flowers bring a gentle almond flavor. Try adding to jams and preserves. The aromatic herb is popular in potpourri and was often used to flavor liquids such as wine, cordials, and vinegars. Meadowsweet tea is said to cure headaches. In the garden, it will attract bees.

Native to Europe and Asia, the wetland-loving perennial is also called queen of the meadow, meadow queen, pride of the meadow, meadsweet, mead wort, lady of the meadow, bridewort, and Quaker lady. The plant's white flowers, true to its name, give off a sweet almond smell. Once popular for flavoring mead and adding to bridal bouquets, meadowsweet was considered one of the most sacred herbs by the Druids of ancient Celtic cultures. Meadowsweet was often scattered on floors in the Middle Ages to freshen the air. It has been discovered in burial sites as far back as the Bronze Age.

In 1897, German chemist Felix Hoffmann produced modified version of salicin made from meadowsweet flowers. Hoffman's employer Bayer AG christened the new medicine aspirin, drawing on the plant's botanical name, *Spiraea ulmaria.*

Green Beans Almondine with Meadowsweet

YIELD
—
Serves 4 as a side dish

1   pound green beans, topped and tailed
1   tablespoon butter
1   shallot, minced
½   cup sliced almonds
    Salt and freshly ground pepper
½   cup meadowsweet blossoms

Bring 2 inches of water to boil in a medium saucepan. Add the green beans, lower the heat, and steam until crisp-tender, 3 to 5 minutes. While they are steaming, melt the butter in a large skillet. When the butter foams, add the shallot and sauté until translucent. Add the almonds and continue to sauté, tossing frequently so the almonds brown a bit but don't burn.

Drain the green beans, add to the skillet, and toss in the butter-shallot mixture to coat. Top with a sprinkle of salt, pepper, and the meadowsweet blossoms.

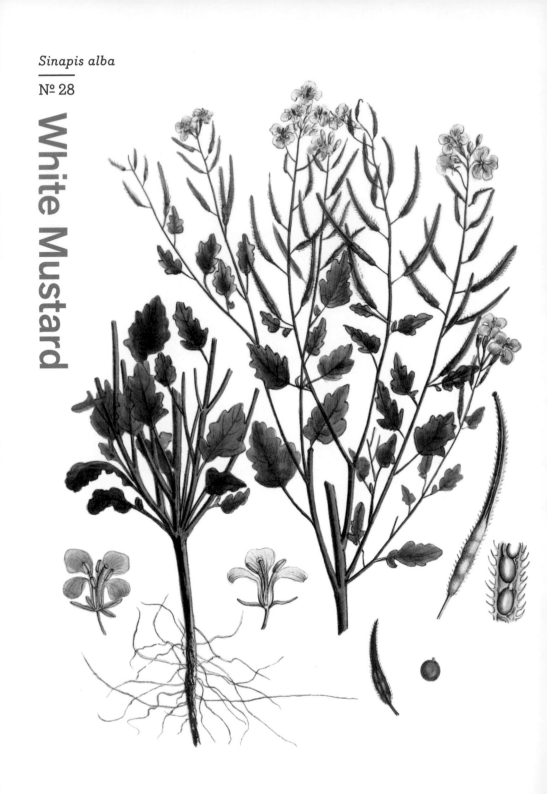

White Mustard

In the language of flowers, mustard seeds symbolize indifference.

TO GROW

Mustard prefers sun or partial shade and does not tolerate dry stretches because the roots are shallow. Grows fast and easily from seed. Spread out seedlings and keep the area well weeded. Greens are best harvested when young. Harvest seeds just before they turn ripe.

USAGE

Use whole mustard seeds for pickling, or grind them and mix with vinegar, salt, honey, and turmeric to make yellow table mustard. Mustard oil is produced by pressing the seeds. The greens can be consumed raw, sautéed with garlic and red pepper flakes, and enjoyed in soups and stews. Mustard seeds can also be made into a facial scrub or mask. Grind seeds, mix with warm water, and leave on skin for no more than fifteen minutes, trying a small test area on your arm before applying to your face. Mustard has also found use as a fodder crop for animals and as a green manure.

White mustard, also called wild mustard, is native to the Mediterranean and belongs to the same family as broccoli and Brussels sprouts. Texts dating back to ancient Sumerian and Sanskrit cultures from 3000 BC record use of the fast-growing annual. Sumerians created an early version of the condiment we know as mustard by mixing juice from unripe grapes with ground mustard seeds. The seeds were also valued by ancient Egyptians, who made sure King Tutankhamun had a supply in his tomb on the way to the next life. The bulk of the world's seed comes from Canada and Nepal. The yellow flowers of the plant create seedpods with approximately six seeds in each.

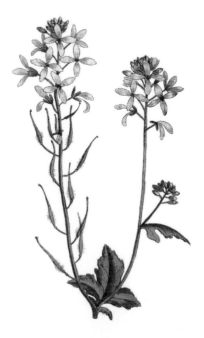

Japanese-Style White Mustard

Try using this mustard instead of Dijon in a classic green salad, with some julienned carrots for color and crunch.

YIELD

Makes about ¾ cup

- ½ cup mustard seeds
- ½ cup sake
- ⅓ cup rice vinegar
- 1 tablespoon sugar
- 1 tablespoon white miso

Mix all the ingredients in a bowl. Cover and steep in the refrigerator for 2 to 3 days. Pour the mixture in a blender and blend until smooth and a little grainy. Add 1 tablespoon of rice vinegar to the mustard if it is too thick. If it is still too thick, add 1 tablespoon of water. This mustard will last up to 6 months in an airtight jar.

Nasturtium

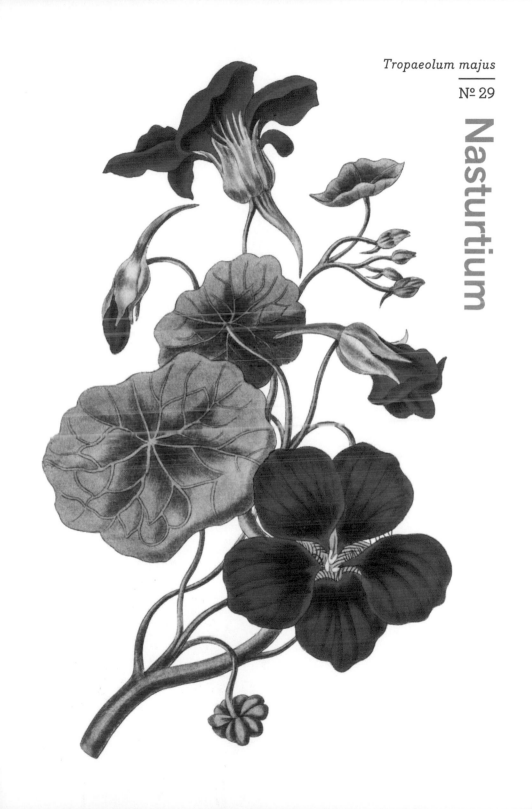

In the language of flowers,
nasturtium means patriotism.

TO GROW

These cheerful annuals are easy to grow and should not be overwatered. They prefer full sun but do not tolerate hot stretches well. If they wilt in heat, trimming them back should help restore them. Nasturtiums work well to cover ground where soil is poor and will grow well alongside broccoli, cucumbers, radishes, and squash.

USAGE

Both flowers and leaves are edible; flowers add a festive color to salads. The flowers are delicious stuffed with cream cheese or ricotta and they work wonderfully for attracting butterflies to the garden.

Also called Indian cress, monk's cress, and Capuchin cress, nasturtium plants are native to Peru and Chile. They're recognizable by the bright red, orange, and yellow flowers that caught the eye of Matisse and Monet.

Spanish botanist Nicolás Monardes brought the plant from South America to Spain in 1569. It was a Swedish botanist—Carl Linnaeus—who named it, inspired by the shield-like shape of the leaves and red flowers, which resemble helmets covered with blood.

The peppery taste is reminiscent of watercress (*Nasturtium officinale*), hence the alternate names with versions of "cress." The pungency likely inspired the name *nasturtium*, meaning nose-twisted, from the Latin *nasum*, nose, and *torquere*, meaning to twist.

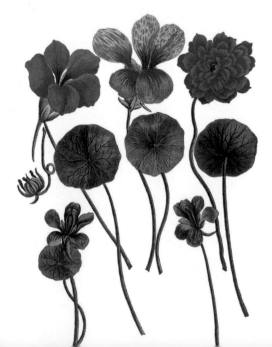

Jewel Mix Cocktail

Nasturtiums are usually thought of as a salad ingredient or food garnish, but the peppery flavor is a natural fit with agave spirits, especially because the genus is native from Mexico to South America.

Makes one cocktail

5 to 6 nasturtium leaves
1 thin slice jalapeño pepper
2 ounces 100% agave blanco tequila
¾ ounce freshly squeezed lime juice
½ ounce grapefruit liqueur (you can substitute equal amounts fresh grapefruit juice and simple syrup, or top the finished drink with grapefruit soda)
¼ ounce agave syrup

Muddle the nasturtium leaves and pepper in a cocktail shaker. Add the tequila, lime juice, grapefruit liqueur, and agave syrup, fill with ice, and shake until the shaker is frosted. Strain into a chilled rocks glass and garnish with a nasturtium flower.

Origanum vulgare

Nº 30

Oregano

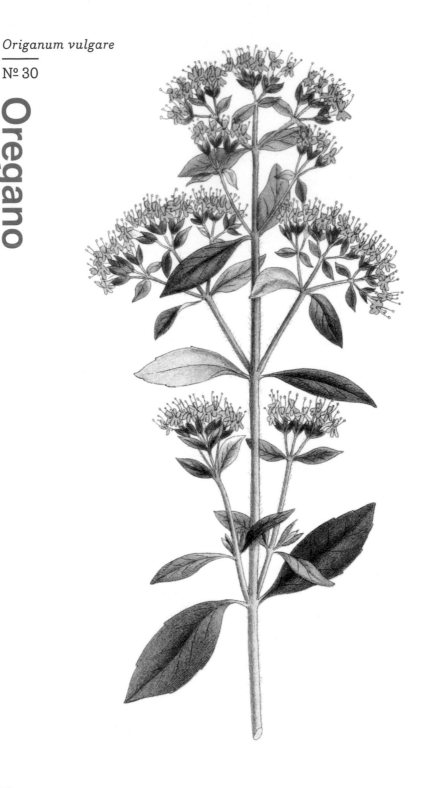

In the language of flowers, oregano represents substance.

TO GROW

Easy to grow from seed; extremely easy all around; lovely flowers; bee attracter; can reach up to 2½ feet in hot, dry climates with well-drained soil. Keep an eye on this perennial—it can take over the garden. Leaves will be most flavorful if harvested just before flowers bloom. Freeze or dry for later use.

USAGE

A staple of Italian cooking, oregano is used in a range of meat, fish, and vegetable dishes, and considered essential to many tomato sauces. Popular in spicy foods prized in southern Italian cuisine. Add to roasted eggplant and zucchini and try in egg dishes. Valued in Turkish and Middle Eastern cooking as well, particularly for flavoring meat. An essential spice along with thyme and marjoram in the Middle Eastern spice mix za'atar. In Greece it is used to flavor lamb and moussaka. The aromatic leaves are sometimes selected for potpourri and dried flower arrangements.

This flowering plant in the mint family, native to the Mediterranean, is also called winter sweet, pizza herb, wild marjoram, Greek oregano, and rigani. The genus name comes from Greek words that mean brightness of the mountain or joy of the mountains. Many varieties of oregano have been cultivated, featuring a variety of flavors from sweet to spicy. Oregano is typically used in its dry form. After World War II, US soldiers brought home a fondness for the "pizza herb" and it was quickly adopted in their homeland. It produces pale purple flowers. (The Mexican oregano typically found in Central American cuisine is from a different plant.)

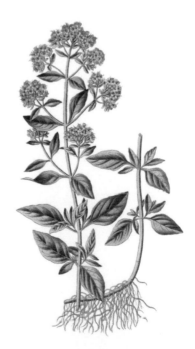

Spiced Olives Appetizer with Dried Oregano

For an authentic Greek experience, serve this appetizer with a glass of ouzo.

YIELD

3½ cups, 10 servings

- **2** cups pitted Kalamata or Moroccan olives
- **1** tablespoon dried oregano, coarsely chopped
- **½** cup sundried tomatoes in oil, drained and minced
- **1** garlic clove, minced
- **1** teaspoon Aleppo pepper
- **1** cup crumbled feta cheese

Place all the ingredients in a a bowl and toss well. Serve with toasted pita wedges.

Parsley

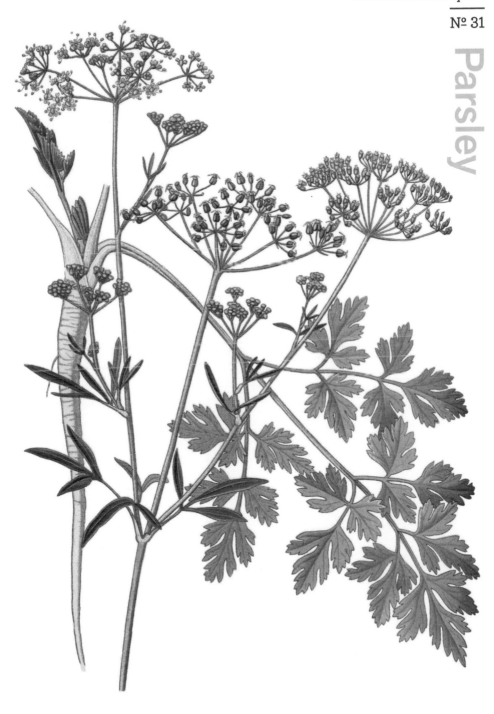

TO GROW

Grow parsley in full sun with moist soil that is kept well drained. Seeds will take a month to a month and a half at least to germinate. Soaking in warm water for a full day will improve growth. Curly parsley grows 12 to 18 inches and makes an attractive ornamental plant. Flat-leaf parsley will grow to between 2 and 3 feet. A good companion for roses in the garden, it is also helpful to tomatoes and asparagus. Preserve by mincing and mixing in a small amount of water first.

USAGE

Combined with chervil, chives, and tarragon, parsley is one of the herbs in the celebrated French mix of *fines herbes* as well as the *bouquet garni*. Combined with garlic, it also makes up part of (and gives its name to) the French persillade sauce, and in the similar Italian gremolata it's mixed with lemon and garlic. Flat-leaf parsley is a favorite in salads, soups, and stews, and works best added near the end of the preparation. The most flavor is found in the stems. Roasted potatoes with butter and parsley make a pleasing side dish. Add it to chicken dishes, fish, sauces, and salad dressings; pair it with garlic

Parsley is a member of a carrot family, native to the rocky cliffs of the Mediterranean. The name comes from the Greek word *petros*, meaning rock. The flowers are small but carry a strong aroma. Greeks and Romans valued it highly, considering it interchangeable with celery. For the Greeks parsley was sacred; they used it as an adornment for tombs and to fashion wreaths of honor. The Romans wore it at feasts, believing it would soak up the smell of other foods. Chewing leaves after a meal has long thought to freshen the breath, a custom that led to parsley's popularity as a garnish.

The three most common types of the plant are curly leaf parsley (*Petroselinum crispum*), also known as French parsley; Italian or flat-leaf parsley (*Petroselinum crispum* var. *neapolitanum*); and Hamburg (*Petroselinum crispum* var. *tuberosum*). It is essential to many cuisines, especially French and Italian.

for a variation to chimichurri or pesto. It's lovely sprinkled over risotto or pasta. The French *bouquet garni* relies on parsley as well as thyme, bay leaf, and other herbs. In the garden, parsley attracts butterflies, is a host plant for anise swallowtail and, when in bloom, honeybees.

Gremolata

This condiment is an essential component of the classic Milanese dish osso buco, but its salty, slightly bitter tang also adds depth to egg dishes, chicken, fish, and grilled or steamed vegetables.

YIELD

Makes ½ cup

1	large bunch Italian parsley, washed and dried
	Zest and juice of 1 lemon
1	garlic clove
¼	cup olive oil
1	teaspoon salt

Place all the ingredients in a food processor and pulse to a texture you like, from coarse to almost a puree.

It will last in the fridge for up to 3 days.

Peppermint

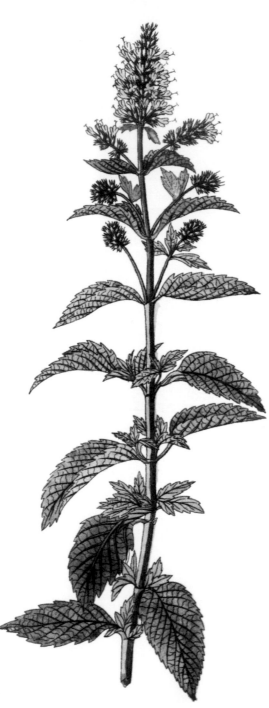

In the Japanese language of flowers, peppermint means warmth of feeling.

TO GROW

Reaching 1 to 3 feet, peppermint grows well in moist habitats with shade or partial sun. As a hybrid, it is typically sterile, spreading by roots and not through any seed production. In the Great Lakes area, it is now considered invasive. Containers are recommended to inhibit rapid spread. The leaves and flowering tops can be harvested as flowers begin to open. Dry for later use.

USAGE

Leaves can be eaten in salads, made into pesto, or used as a garnish for fruit. Try with red wine vinegar and garlic as a substitute for cilantro in chimichurri. Steep leaves in hot water for tea. Peppermint is also used for flavoring ice cream, toothpaste, mouthwash, soaps, candy, cosmetics, and skin lotions, as well as dandruff shampoos and various aromatherapy treatments. The cooling effect when applied topically makes it popular for itchiness relief.

This perennial herb is sweet and pungent, a cross between wintergreen and spearmint. Native to the Middle East and Europe, it was used to combat indigestion in ancient Egypt and valued by the ancient Greeks and Romans as well. The hybrid herb was also mentioned in the Bible. A range of varieties offer different scents, including fruit flavors like lemon, orange, and lime as well as chocolate and lavender. The species name *piperita* comes from the Latin word for pepper. Oregon and Washington are the biggest peppermint producers in the US today, with much of this supply devoted to making essential oils.

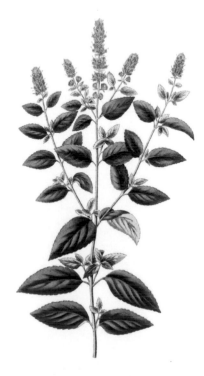

Chocolate Peppermint Leaves

These leaves make delicious garnishes for all manner of desserts, from peppermint ice cream to chocolate cupcakes.

YIELD

Makes 20 leaves

- **1** ounce fine dark chocolate (at least 70% cacao), broken into small pieces
- **1** teaspoon coconut oil
- **20** large fresh peppermint leaves

Melt the chocolate and coconut oil in a small bowl in the microwave in 30-second intervals, stirring after each microwave session. Using a pastry brush, brush the bottom halves of both sides of the mint leaves with the melted chocolate. Place the leaves on wax paper to harden for about 1 hour.

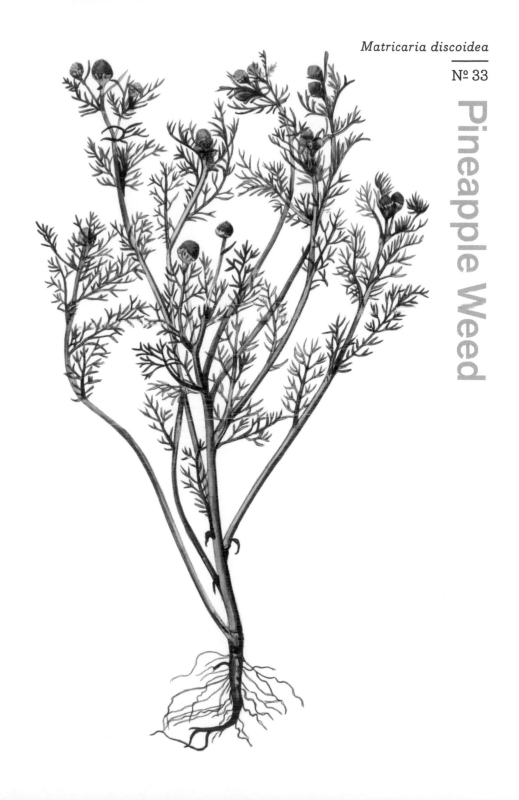

Pineapple Weed

Pineapple weed was one of the botanicals Meriwether Lewis collected on the Clearwater River in 1805 during the Lewis and Clark Expedition.

TO GROW

Will grow to 1 foot. Often found along roadsides, preferring soil that is frequently turned over. From seed, it will grow to produce seed in approximately 100 days. Its abundance is often tied to increased traffic, which helps spread the seed via tires. Removing the flowers increases growth.

USAGE

Foragers sometimes enjoy pineapple weed flowers and leaves, which can also be added to salads. Dried and crushed, the flowers can be used as a type of flour. Makes a pleasant tea or simple syrup. Can be added to baked goods such as cookies, as well as jams, liquors, and cordials.

Pineapple weed is also known as wild chamomile, false chamomile, disc mayweed, and street weed. Native to northeastern Asia, it often grows in the wild. The Latin genus name comes from the words for mother (*matria*) and dear (*caria*). It resembles its bigger cousin chamomile, with which it often gets confused. Can be distinguished by the lack of flower petals and the smell of pineapple released when crushed.

The Crow or Absaroka people indigenous to North America used pineapple weed in a variety of ways, from weaving into rugs and mats to lining cradles. For the Inuit, it is an incense and indicator of seasons, a food preservative (crushed into powder) for the Flathead people, and a perfume for the Kutenai and Blackfoot. The yellowish-green cone heads are enjoyed as a treat by children in some of these tribes.

Tropic of Pineapple Cocktail

The subtle grassy flavor of this herb gives
a classic rum cocktail a sophisticated twist.

YIELD
—

Makes 1 cocktail

2 ounces Pineapple Weed Rum
(recipe follows)
1 slice fresh pineapple
Wedge of lime

Pour Pineapple Weed Rum over ice and garnish with
the fruit.

Pineapple Weed Rum

YIELD

Makes about 1½ cups

- ¾ cup fresh pineapple weed flowers and leaves
- 2 slices fresh pineapple, chopped
- 1½ cups (12 ounces) white rum
- 3 tablespoons agave

Put ½ cup of the fresh pineapple weed and the chopped pineapple in a clean glass quart jar with a cover. Pour in the rum, cover, and shake vigorously. Put the remaining ¼ cup of the pineapple weed in a small glass jam jar. Pour the agave over it and cover the jar.

Place both jars on a sunny windowsill or porch for 6 to 8 hours.

Strain the agave pineapple weed mixture through a fine-mesh sieve into a 1-quart jar. Using the same sieve, strain the infused rum into the jar. The rum will dissolve any remaining agave on its way through. Transfer to a bottle and cork or seal tightly.

Purslane

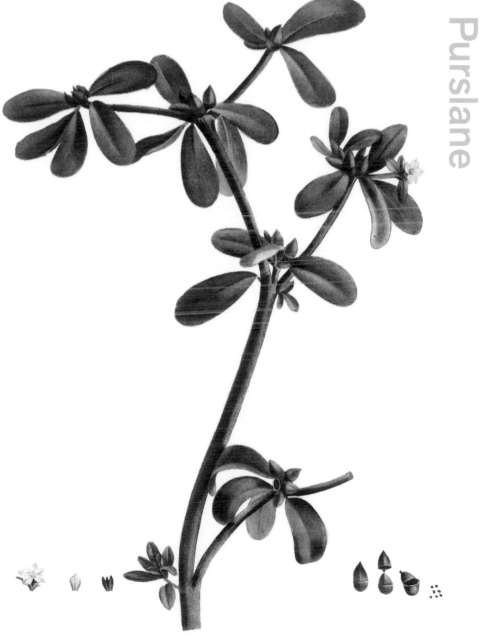

Purslane, also called parsley, pigweed, duckweed, fatweed, verdolagas, and hogweed, is an herb native to India and Persia and is especially popular in Mediterranean cooking. The annual succulent has spread worldwide and is often thought of as a weed. It looks similar to a miniature jade plant, with bright yellow flowers and red stems. Purslane is approximately 93% water.

TO GROW

Grow in full sun, leaving seeds uncovered when planting. Purslane tolerates drought and thrives in most soil types. It is adaptive and needs very little care once it starts growing. The important thing is to keep up a regular harvesting process, ideally before flowering, so it does not invade the garden.

USAGE

Purslane is compared in taste to spinach and watercress and can be used raw or cooked in place of either. Some note its lemony and peppery overtones. High in vitamins C and A as well omega-3 fatty acids, it pairs well with feta cheese. Although you would have to eat a large amount of purslane to accumulate a significant amount, this herb does have a concentration of oxalic acid, which can exacerbate urinary complaints. The leaves and stems can be blanched for a few minutes in hot water then served with a sprinkle of olive oil and grated cheese. Chopped purslane leaves can also be used in the Argentinian condiment chimichurri, which is served with grilled meats.

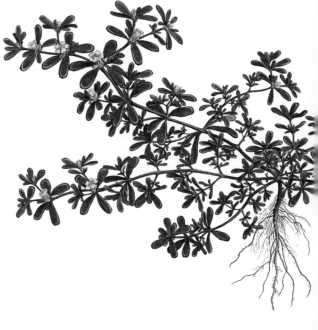

Purslane Salad

Serves 4

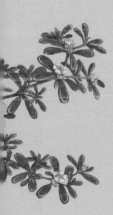

1	red onion, sliced thin
¼	cup red wine vinegar
	Salt
	Sugar
1	cucumber, diced
4	plum tomatoes, diced
1	pound purslane, leaves and tender stems coarsely chopped
3	tablespoons olive oil
1	teaspoon dried oregano
¼	cup feta cheese, crumbled

Mix the red onion with the vinegar and a pinch each of salt and sugar in a large bowl. Let this sit for 15 minutes while you chop the cucumber, tomatoes, and purslane. Add the remaining ingredients to the bowl and toss to combine.

Rhubarb

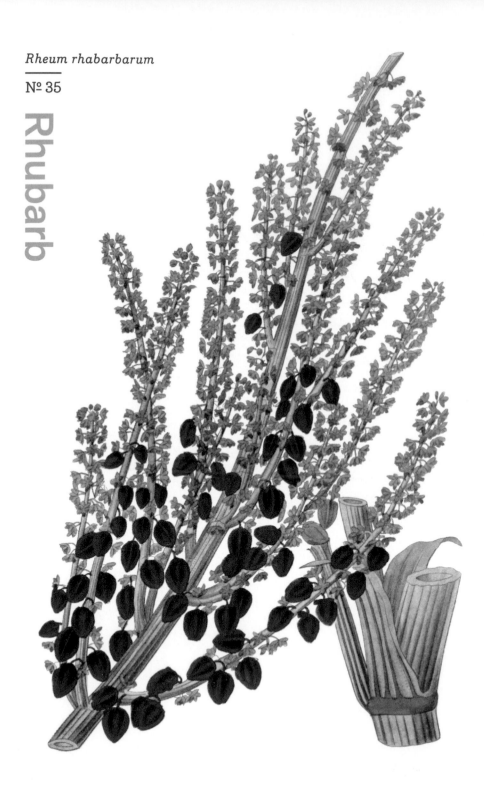

In the Victorian language of flowers, rhubarb stands for advice.

TO GROW

Rhubarb grows easily in fertile, well-drained soils. Rather than starting from seed, most choose to start new plants with division. Cover the crowns with a small amount of soil, and water thoroughly. Shortly after the leaf expands is the best time to harvest for tastiest stalks.

USAGE

Rhubarb stalks resemble celery but are very tart eaten raw. Cook with sugar for pies, jams, and other treats. You can also stew it to make jam and compotes. Rhubarb and strawberries are a favorite combination. High in vitamin C, fiber, and calcium, rhubarb can be combined with apples, sugar, and oats for a variation on apple crisp, and it makes a tart, refreshing chilled soup with strawberries. In England it is often served with whipped cream or custard. It can also be enjoyed as a punch or tonic and as an ingredient in wine and mead.

This cool-weather perennial is now classified as a vegetable (because in China it was used historically as a medicinal herb). Its crispy stalks, however, are enjoyed as fruit, a springtime favorite cooked in pies and other baked goods. The leaves are poisonous, however. Ripening early in the season, rhubarb is one of the first plants harvested for food in temperate climates. Washington State produces half the rhubarb consumed in the US.

In China, rhubarb has been used for medicinal purposes for more than 2,000 years. It was carried along the Silk Road and became highly valued in Europe. Thomas Jefferson planted it in his Monticello garden.

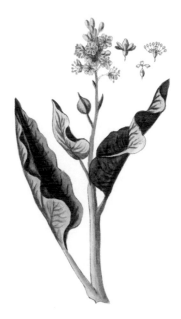

Long Red Jacket Cocktail

YIELD
—
Makes 1 cocktail

2 ounces apple brandy or apple eau de vie
1 ounce freshly squeezed lemon juice (save some of the peel for garnish)
¼ ounce orange liqueur
¼ ounce Orgeat (almond-flavored syrup)
1 heaping teaspoon Rhubarb Puree, or more to taste (recipe opposite)

Add all the ingredients to a cocktail shaker with ice, and shake until the shaker is frosted. Strain into a chilled cocktail glass. Twist a lemon peel over the glass and discard the peel.

Rhubarb Puree

YIELD
___
1½ cups puree

1 pound rhubarb stalks, cut into ½-inch pieces,
peel if they are large and stringy (about 3 cups)

½ cup granulated sugar

½ cup water

½ teaspoon freshly squeezed lemon juice

¼ teaspoon salt

In a medium saucepan over low heat add all the
ingredients. Bring to a boil, then reduce the heat and
simmer until rhubarb has broken down and the mixture
is syrupy (about 10 minutes). Remove from the heat
and cool completely before adding to the cocktail. The
remainder can be spooned over yogurt or ice cream.

Salvia rosmarinus

Nº 36

Rosemary

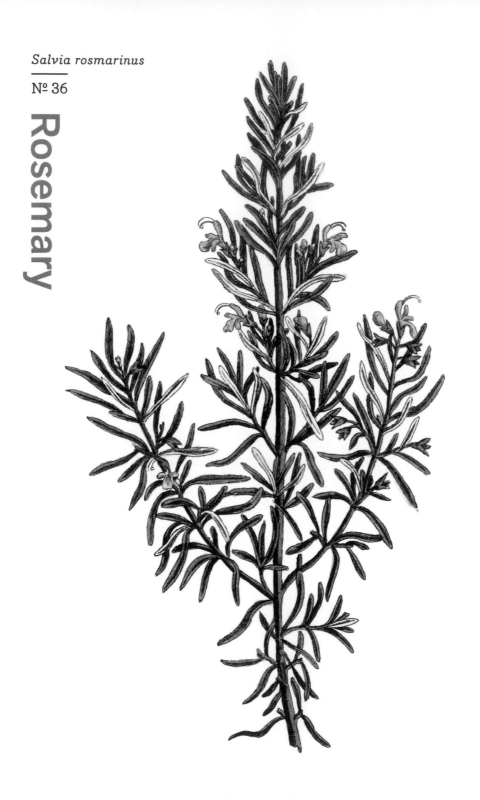

In the Victorian language of flowers, rosemary symbolizes remembrance.

TO GROW

Begin with cuttings and grow in full sun with well-drained soil. The shrub resists pests and tolerates drought easily but is vulnerable to cold weather. Water very little when growing in containers.

USAGE

Rosemary lends its distinct flavor to a range of foods, from breads to roasted meats and vegetables. It makes a novel addition to lemonade. The flowers are edible and can be added to salads or mixed into butter. The branches from a well-established shrub can be soaked and used as skewers when barbecuing. Add leaves to potpourri, dream pillows (sparingly), and sachets. The scent of the leaves repels moths from clothes drawers. The oil is used in perfumes, shampoos, and cleaning products and is said to be stimulating for hair when massaged into scalp. Attracts bees to the garden and can be shaped into topiary.

This perennial shrub, a member of the mint family, is also known as compass weed, compass plant, and polar plant. An earlier name—Rose of Mary—paid tribute to the Virgin Mary. Native to the Mediterranean, rosemary thrives in warm climates, but if established in areas with mild winters it can grow into a huge bush. The leaves are needle-like, with a fragrance resembling pine and a pungent flavor. Small blue or violet flowers grow in clusters, echoing the color of the Virgin Mary's raiment. The Roman name, *rosmarinus*, meaning dew of the sea, is apt: the ancient herb flourishes by the sea. The aromatic plant was documented in cuneiform tablets from 5000 BC.

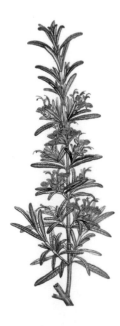

Mushroom Rosemary Pizza

The piney taste of rosemary and the smoky mozzarella give this pizza a distinctly autumnal taste.

YIELD
———
Makes 1 10-inch pizza

Cornmeal for rolling out dough
½ package whole wheat pizza dough
2 tablespoons olive oil
2 cups mixed mushrooms, such as shiitake, portobello, or cremini, sliced thin
1 medium sweet onion, sliced thin
6 ounces smoked mozzarella, shredded
2 sprigs fresh rosemary, chopped, or 1 teaspoon dried
Freshly ground pepper

Preheat oven to 500 degrees.

Sprinkle cornmeal over the counter and roll out pizza
dough until ¼ inch thick. Spread onto oiled pizza pan
or baking sheet. Sprinkle with 1 tablespoon of the
olive oil. Scatter the mushrooms over, then the onion
slices. Drizzle 1 tablespoon of olive oil over mushrooms
and onions. Spread the mozzarella slices on top,
then scatter rosemary over all. Grind pepper over the
surface.

Bake 6 to 8 minutes, until the cheese melts, the
mushrooms and onions soften, and the edges are crisp.

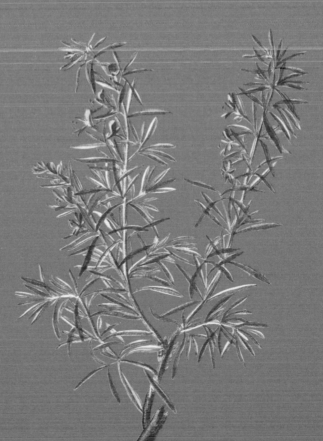

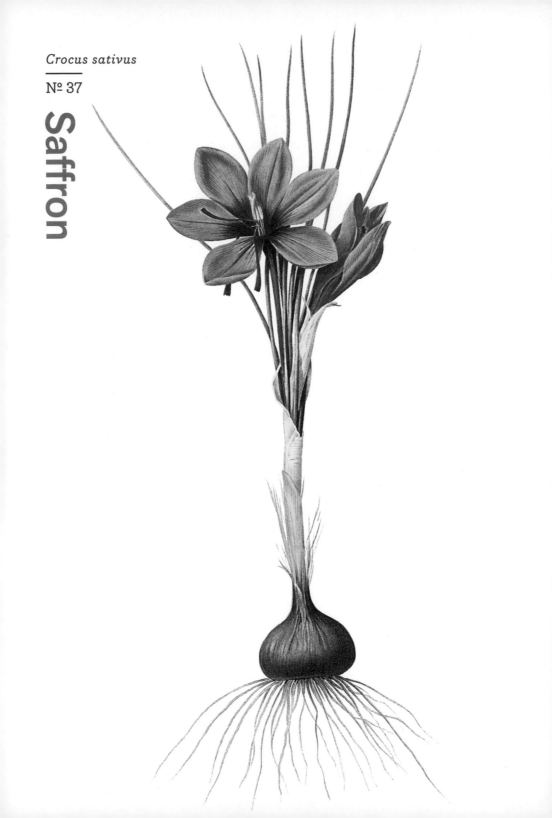

Crocus sativus

№ 37

Saffron

In the Japanese language of flowers, saffron represents mirth.

TO GROW

Saffron doesn't grow in the wild. Plant the bulbs in full sun and sandy soil. Water regularly and keep well drained. Look for blooms in the fall and harvest quickly. Flowers fade during the day. The entire blooming phase will be over in 1 or 2 weeks. Hand-picking the flower is the first step; next you separate the stamen and petals. Use airtight containers to preserve the dried stigma. A single pound of saffron requires 70,000 blooms.

USAGE

Indian, Spanish, Arabic, and Persian cuisines often feature the precious spice, which is also an ingredient in certain confectioneries and liquors. It adds a lovely, unique flavor to risotto, paella, and pastas as well as French bouillabaisse. In India, the color of saffron is thought to bring good luck and is often found in festivals and sacred ceremonies.

Saffron is the world's most expensive spice. The precious seasoning comes from the "saffron crocus"—the flower of *Crocus sativus*. The common name may come from the Arabic *za'faran* or Latin *safaranum*. Each flower yields only three saffron threads. Likely native to Greece or Iran, saffron has a subtle, earthy taste, often described as grass-like or hay-like. Most of the world's supply comes from Iran, although it is also grown in Spain, Greece, Morocco, and India.

In England, Saffron Walden in Essex and Saffron Hill in London recall a time when it was widely grown there. Although the yellow robes of Buddhist monks are described as saffron-colored, they're actually dyed with turmeric, a common substitute for the pricey spice.

These Hours Are Golden Cocktail

Saffron is used in a number of historic herbal liqueurs, such as *amari*, but it's tricky to use as a straight ingredient: too little and the flavor will be lost; too much and the saffron will dominate the drink. Here a tincture is used to elevate the simple gin and tonic to loftier pretensions. You can vary the proportions to taste, but make sure to follow the steps in the right order to achieve maximum flavor and color!

YIELD

Makes 1 cocktail

2 lime wheels, 1 cut near the end so you have more rind than pulp
2 ounces London dry gin
Saffron-Cardamom Tincture (recipe follows)
Tonic water

Muddle the lime wheel from the end of the lime (with more rind) in the bottom of a tall glass. Add gin and about 10 drops tincture and stir a few times. Add ice, top with tonic water to taste, and stir gently once or twice to incorporate. Garnish with the second lime wheel, or squeeze it and drop it in.

Saffron-Cardamom Tincture

YIELD

Makes 1 cup

1   heaping teaspoon green cardamom, or about
    12 pods
1   large pinch saffron threads (use good-quality
    saffron)
4   ounces Everclear or other high-proof vodka
4   ounces water

Crack the cardamom pods in a mortar and pestle; add
the saffron threads and crush lightly. Place spices in a
small glass jar and add the alcohol. Shake to combine
and store in a cool, dark location. Open and sniff it once
a day, the color and fragrance will develop after 2 to
3 days. When ready, strain the solids and add water
to the remaining liquor. Pour into a glass bottle with an
eyedropper top or dropper cap. The same technique,
substituting 8 ounces of hot water and 1 cup of sugar
for the Everclear and water, will make a simple syrup
instead.

Sage

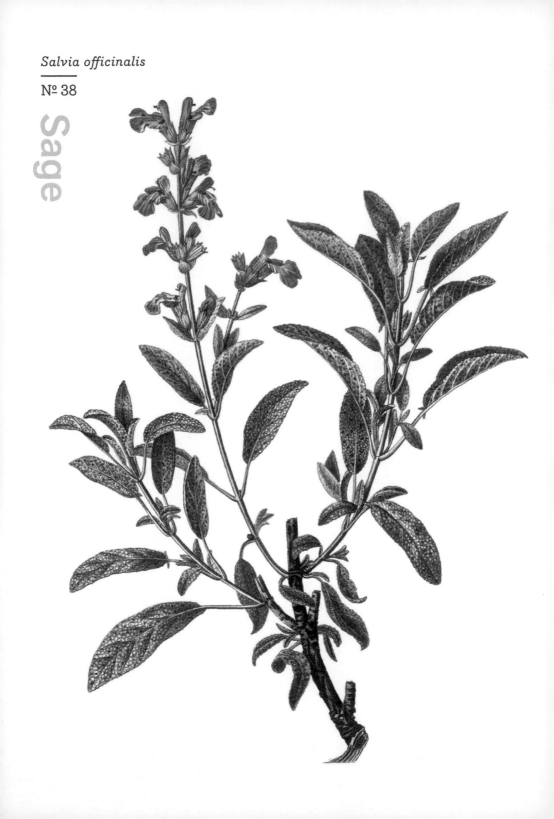

In the Victorian language of flowers, sage stands for domestic virtue.

An evergreen member of the mint family, sage also goes by a host of more descriptive names such as kitchen sage, garden sage, true sage, common sage, culinary sage, and Dalmatian sage. The perennial shrub's leaves are gray-green. One side is covered with soft pale fuzz that makes the leaves unappealing in raw form. Its flowers vary from a lavender to deep purple. Flowers, though musky-smelling, are very beautiful and complex in color and pattern. Native to the Balkans region, the origin of the genus name is the Latin *salvere*, to heal or save. Albania is one of the world's biggest producers.

TO GROW

Grow from cuttings in full sun and well-drained soil. Will reach 2 feet. Tolerates drought. Its long season and tolerance for a variety of temperatures makes it popular for indoors. Harvest early in the day, when dew is just dry.

USAGE

Sage's pungent, peppery flavor with a slight minty taste is largely retained when dried and is used in stuffings, soups, bean dishes, and sausage. A sage-flavored cheese is popular in England, as is a butter-lemon sauce for pasta in Italy. Another Italian dish that relies on sage is saltimbocca. The leaves can be fried and made into chips. Sage also has spiritual properties. Native Americans have a long tradition of burning sage in a purification and cleansing ritual meant to attract positive energy. It is an ingredient in antiperspirants and skin creams and stimulates the scalp and conditions the hair.

According to manuscripts from the Middle Ages, a common hand wash and tooth powder both incorporated sage, and during the Great Plague, the herb was one of those said to offer protection. Renaissance cookbooks include a cold sauce made of sage.

Sage Tomato Pasta

This delicate tomato pasta topped with fried sage leaves is superb in summer with fresh tomatoes but also very good in winter using canned tomatoes. Sage leaves stay green well after the first frost.

YIELD

———

Makes 6 servings

1	white onion, chopped coarsely
¼	cup plus 2 tablespoons olive oil
2	garlic cloves, minced
2	pounds ripe tomatoes, chopped coarsely, or 1 2-pound can San Marzano tomatoes
	Salt and pepper
2	cups sage leaves
	Flour for dusting
1	pound dried spaghetti or thin linguine
	Grated Parmesan cheese, for serving

Preheat oven to 300 degrees.

Sauté the onions in 2 tablespoons of olive oil until translucent. Add the garlic and sauté another minute or so, but don't let the garlic brown. Add the tomatoes, bring to a boil, then reduce heat and simmer for 20 minutes, until sauce thickens. Taste for salt and pepper and add as needed.

While the sauce is cooking, place the sage leaves in a bowl and dust with flour. Heat ¼ cup oil in a flat-bottom pan until it sizzles when you drop a sage leaf in. Fry the sage leaves in batches, transferring to a piece of parchment paper on a baking sheet. Store in the warm oven.

Bring a pot of salted water to boil. Cook the spaghetti until al dente (around 8 minutes), drain, and add to tomato sauce. Add the remaining oil that was used to fry sage leaves and toss.

Top each plate with handfuls of the fried sage leaves. Serve with Parmesan.

Tragopogon porrifolius

Nº 39

Salsify

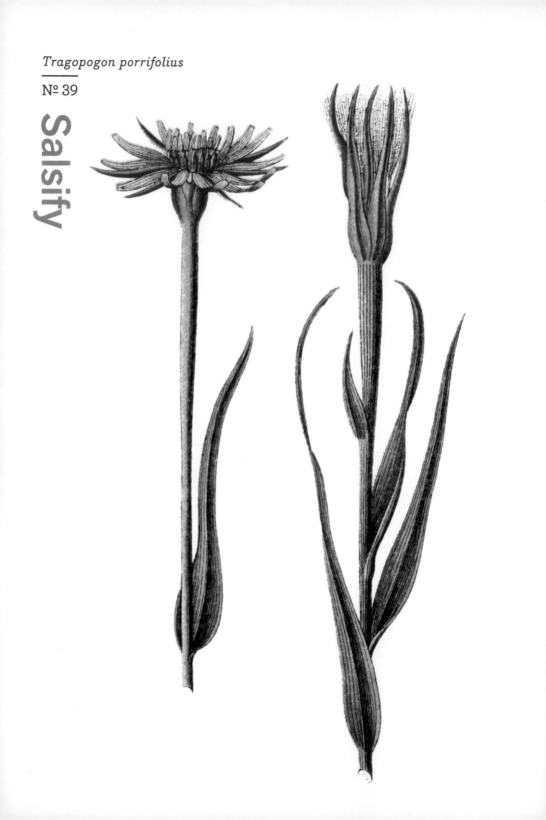

Salsify flowers point toward the sun and follow it in the sky; the name comes from the Latin solsequium, *meaning sol or sun; and* sequens, *or following.*

TO GROW

Growing to 4 feet, salsify thrives in cool weather and well-drained soil that is kept moist. It flowers from April to July, and you'll see the puffy white flower heads when they turn to seed, similar to that of a huge dandelion. Flowers are open in the morning when there is enough sun. Harvest before frost and use promptly.

USAGE

All parts of the plant are edible. Roots provide iron, vitamin C, calcium, potassium, and antioxidants. Some people extract latex from the roots to make chewing gum. Harvesting in late spring, when the plant is still young, is best when using raw in salads. More mature roots can be added to soups and stews or roasted or sautéed. Use in place of artichoke hearts (the taste is somewhat similar) or prepare with butter, cheese, and a little flour for a variation on scalloped potatoes. For a fast, simple preparation, sauté together with greens in butter.

This native to Europe and Africa also goes by meadow salsify, purple salsify, yellow salsify, goatsbeard, shepherd's clock, noon flower, Jack-go-to-bed-at-noon, and star of Jerusalem. A member of the sunflower family, salsify is often found growing in meadows, fields, and roadsides, as well as places where soil is frequently turned over.

Two plants are called salsify. They're different species, but both have a long, narrow carrot-like root with a flower resembling a daisy. "True" salsify (*Tragopogon porrifolius*), or oyster plant, has a purple flower and a white root. False salsify (*Scorzonera hispanica*), black salsify, or Spanish salsify, has yellow flower and a black root. Both are edible and can be prepared the same way.

Salsify Chips

YIELD
———
Serves 4

1 ½ pounds white or black salsify roots
      Flour for dusting
¼   cup olive oil
¼   teaspoon sea salt
      Freshly ground pepper
      Juice of ½ lemon

Rinse and scrub salsify under running water. Peel
with a vegetable peeler and rinse again. Cut into 3-inch
pieces about ¼ inch thick. Blanch in salted boiling
water until just tender, about 3 minutes. Remove from
water and pat dry.

Tip the salsify pieces into a bowl, dust with flour,
and toss until all are lightly coated. Heat the oil in a
large skillet over medium-high heat. Add salsify pieces
in batches and cook until browned and crisp, flipping
pieces as needed. Sprinkle with salt and pepper.
Serve with a squeeze of lemon.

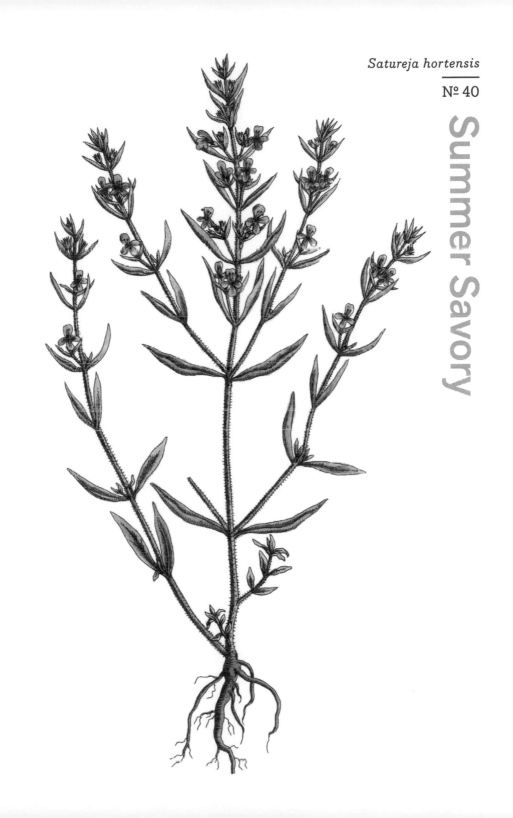

Summer Savory

In the language of flowers,
savory means spice or interest.

TO GROW
Grow savory in full sun and in well-drained soil. Plants will reach 2 feet and tolerate cold well. Seeds grow slowly. Harvest when the plants are flowering and dry for later use.

USAGE
Romans used savory as a salt substitute. Today in Bulgaria it is mixed with salt and paprika and sometimes thyme and fenugreek to make a cherished spice called *sharena sol*, or colorful salt. Savory is often included in the celebrated French mixture *herbes de Provence*. It complements bean dishes with a smoky note and enhances a range of meats, fish dishes, and stews. Winter savory helps preserve salami and can be added to stuffings and herb cheeses or used to infuse oil. Summer savory pairs well with garlic to flavor green beans.

The genus *Satureja* includes numerous species of herbs or shrubs, all but one native to the Mediterranean and the Middle East. Of these, two are commonly grown: winter and summer savory. Winter is the hardier plant, with subtle, earthy tones. Before the spice trade from Asia introduced black pepper, it was widely used in Europe. Winter savory gets its species name, *montana*, or mountain, from its association with rocky settings. Summer savory has a more pungent and peppery taste. Both have hints of mint and thyme. The plant inspired the description of food as "savory," meaning flavorful.

The ancient Romans thought savory was an aphrodisiac and made love potions out of it. The "herb of love" was forbidden in the gardens of European monasteries, presumably to protect against the monks falling under its enchantment.

Savory Lentil Stew

A simple yet nourishing soup that tastes even better the day after it is made.

2 to 3 tablespoons olive oil
1 red onion, peeled and chopped
3 to 4 garlic cloves, finely chopped
2 large carrots, chopped
2 stalks celery, chopped
4 cups vegetable stock
2 cups brown lentils
1 tablespoon fresh winter savory leaves, whole
1 bunch Swiss chard, washed and sliced across the leaves and stems
1 teaspoon sherry vinegar

Heat the olive oil in a large pot over medium-high heat. Add the onion and sauté until translucent.

Add the garlic, carrots, and celery to the pot, and stir well to combine. Cook for 3 to 4 minutes.

                     Recipe continues on next page

Add the stock, lentils, and savory. Season with salt and pepper. Bring to a boil, then reduce heat and cover the pot. After 15 minutes, add the Swiss chard, cover, and cook another 5 to 10 minutes, until the lentils are soft and the chard stems are tender. Remove from heat, and stir in the sherry vinegar.

Serve with whole-grain toast.

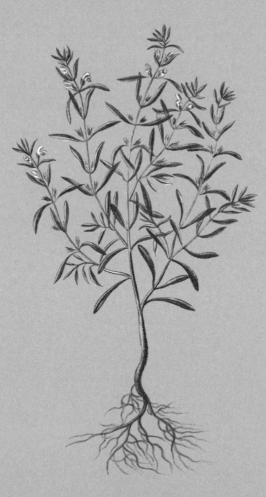

Pelargonium spp.

№ 41

Scented Geranium

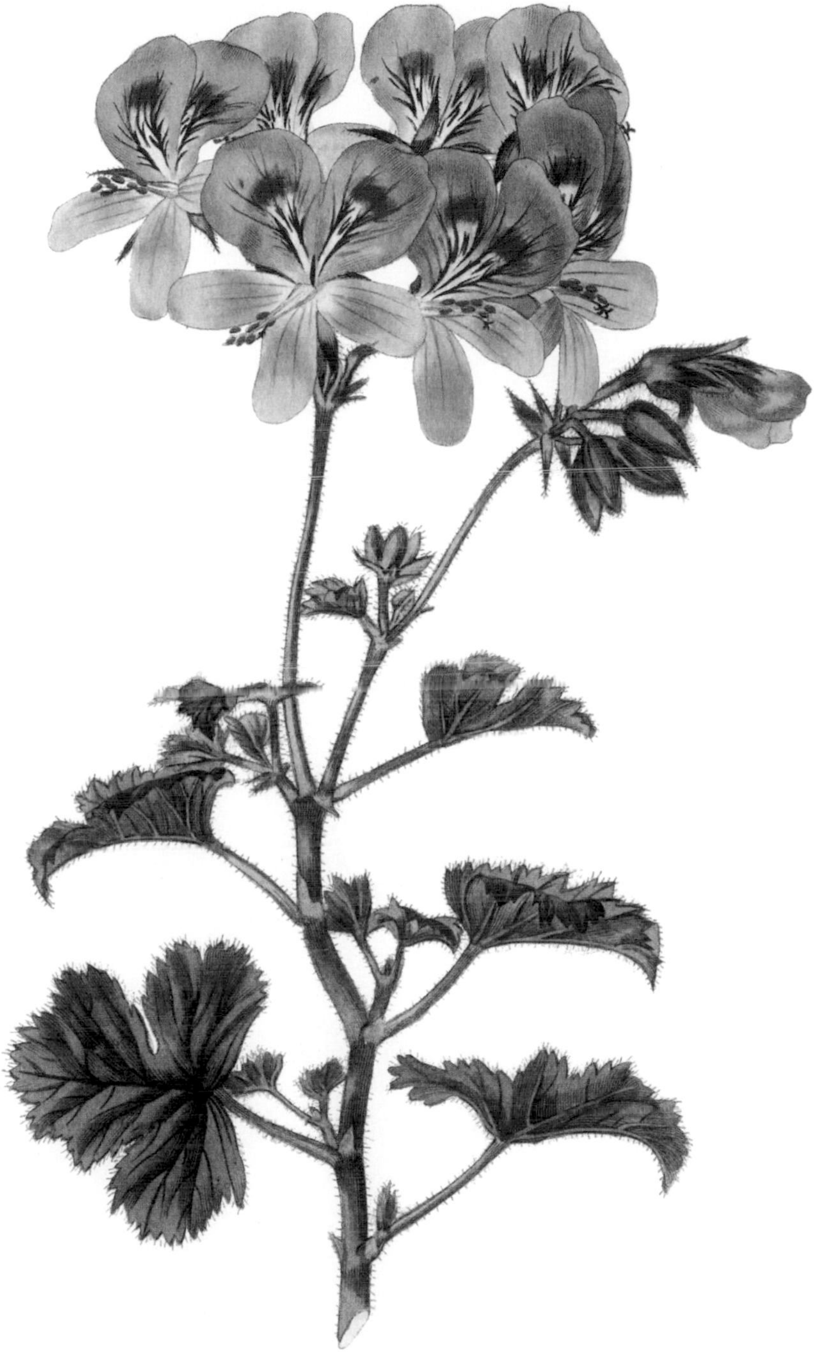

In the Victorian language of flowers, the geranium symbolized foolishness or stupidity.

TO GROW
Popular as indoor plants, where they can fare well with poor light. Outside, scented geraniums thrive in full sun or partial shade. Keep soil moist and well drained. To grow more so you can replicate the scent you want, take cuttings above the leaf nodule and begin them in water. When roots grow, plant in soil. Plants will grow to 1 to 3 feet indoors. Outside they can grow considerably larger.

USAGE
Victorian gardeners made fragrant finger bowls by floating the leaves in water. They can be used to flavor jellies, sorbets, vinegars, fruit punches, lemonades, and perfumes. Geranium-sweetened sugar is an interesting alternative to vanilla in tea biscuits, pound cake, and shortbread.

While flowering geraniums are adored for their bright blooms, scented geraniums are celebrated for their aroma. Depending on the variety, rubbing the leaves releases a wonderland of scents, including lemon, strawberry, pineapple, apricot, apple, rose, cinnamon, cloves, nutmeg, pine, honey, chocolate, and coconut. Tender perennials with tiny flowers, scented geraniums have highly concentrated essential oils in their cells. They are native to South Africa, and English and Dutch sailors brought them to Europe. They appeared in the US in the middle of the eighteenth century.

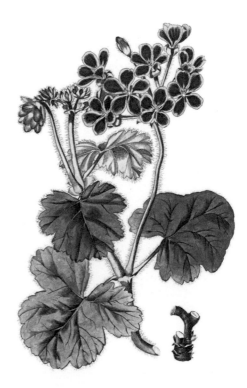

Scented Geranium Oil

This spicy scented oil has multiple uses. Comb it into your hair as conditioner (rinsing after a few minutes), or smooth it on your hands and feet to soothe dry skin.

To make scented geranium oil, pick a handful of geranium leaves, chop them, and pound in a mortar with ¼ cup sugar. Fill a jar with a cup of neutral oil (avocado or safflower) and add the pulverized leaves. Shake the jar vigorously before using.

Scented Towels

Scented geranium leaves of your choosing make a wonderful surprise when wrapped in warm, damp hand towels and passed around at the end of a meal.

Sesame

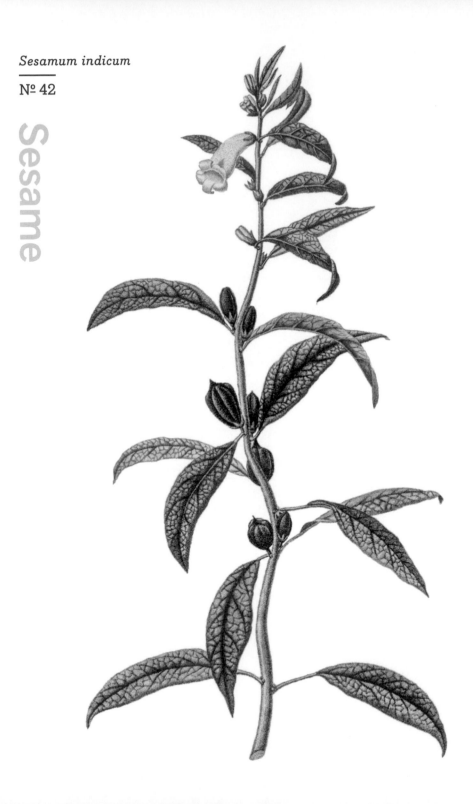

*Hindu legend associates
sesame with immortality.*

TO GROW

Start indoors and transplant once temperature is at least 70 degrees outside. Sesame likes full sun and well-drained soil and will reach at least 3 to 5 feet. White, pink, or lavender flowers will turn into seedpods, which will pop open to reveal the seeds themselves. Harvest when the leaves begin to fall and the seedpods turn brown. Dry in the sun.

USAGE

High in vitamins, protein, and antioxidants, sesame seeds are popular sprinkled on breads, pastries, bagels, buns, and crackers. They can also be enjoyed on salads and used to flavor chicken, tofu, and various vegetable dishes such as eggplant or green beans. In the Middle East, sesame is crushed into tahini, which is combined with chickpeas, garlic, lemon, and oil to make hummus. The Middle Eastern spice blend za'atar mixes sesame with sumac and other spices. Halvah is a candy made with sesame seeds and sugar or honey, popular in the Middle East and especially Israel. The Japanese roll rice in sesame when making sushi rolls. The oil is extremely popular for cooking in China, India, and

This annual native to India and Africa is also known as benne or beniseed. Sesame has now been cultivated in many countries, including the United States, China, and El Salvador, and is used as both a spice and a cooking oil. The seeds range in color from white to brown to black; their nutty flavor is enriched by toasting. One of the oldest cultivated plants, sesame was prized for its oil by ancient Babylonians and ground into flour by ancient Egyptians. Ancient Romans made a spread from the seeds to enjoy on bread. In his travels, Marco Polo noted the use of sesame for oil in South Asia where olive oil was not available. Variants of sesame grew and were traded along the Silk Road. Today China is the world's largest producer.

Egypt. Toasted sesame oil makes a delicious salad dressing. Sesame is also used in cleansers, face masks, skin scrubs, shampoos, bath oils, and lotions. Sesame can, however, trigger an allergic reaction in some people.

Lebanese Za'atar

YIELD
_____

Makes about 2 cups spice mixture

- ½   cup sesame seeds, toasted
- 1   cup dried oregano
- ½   cup sumac spice
- 1   teaspoon salt
- ¼   cup dried thyme

Preheat oven to 350 degrees.

Toast the sesame seeds on a baking sheet for a few minutes. Watch them, as they burn easily. Remove and let cool. Mix with remaining ingredients. Can be stored in a tightly covered jar for up to 6 months.

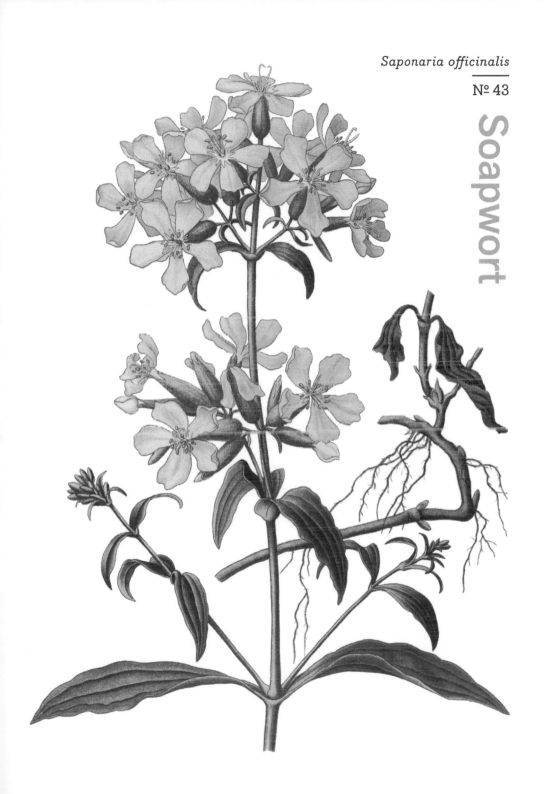

Soapwort once sent a lovely aroma through the streets of London, earning it the nickname London pride.

Native to Europe and Asia, soapwort is also called soapweed, crow soap, Fuller's herb, wild sweet William, lady's washbowl, and bouncing bet. The moniker "bouncing bet" may refer to washerwomen, who were often given the nickname Bets. The perennial has a long history as a soap and detergent. The saponin found in the perennial's leaves and roots creates bubbles, leading to the plant's long history as a soap and detergent. The genus name derives from the Latin *sapo*, soap. The flowers range in color from white to pink, with a smell reminiscent of cloves.

TO GROW

Soapwort prefers full sun or light shade and well-drained, regularly watered soil. It will grow up to 3 feet and should be spaced 1 foot apart. It will self-sow and is not ideal for container gardening because of spreading. Harvest roots in the autumn.

USAGE

A mild cleanser can be made by chopping and boiling soapwort. Although soapwort is typically gentle when used sparingly, some may experience irritation when coming in contact with it. Some use the roots to make a skin wash to help reduce acne and psoriasis or the whole plant to create a hair wash. Halvah is a Middle Eastern treat made with sesame seeds, sugar, and soapwort extract; however, when eaten in large quantities the plant can be toxic, and consumption is not recommended. Attracts pollinators, including bees, hummingbirds, and butterflies, to the garden.

Ancient Assyrians made soap from the perennial herb. Romans used it to soften water, and it appeared later in European wool mills to treat cloth. (The sites of old mills are still recognizable because of the nearby soapwort plants.) Puritans likely introduced soapwort to North America.

Gentle Liquid Soap

You can easily make your own all-natural liquid soap. Mix 1 cup of crushed, loosely packed soapwort leaves with 3 cups of boiling water. Simmer for about 20 minutes over low heat. Allow to cool, then strain.

> **Note:** The soap keeps for only about 1 week, so use it right away. It's a very mild detergent, but to determine if you are allergic, first try washing a spot on your arm or leg.

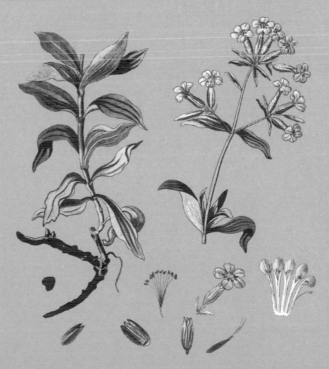

Sorrel

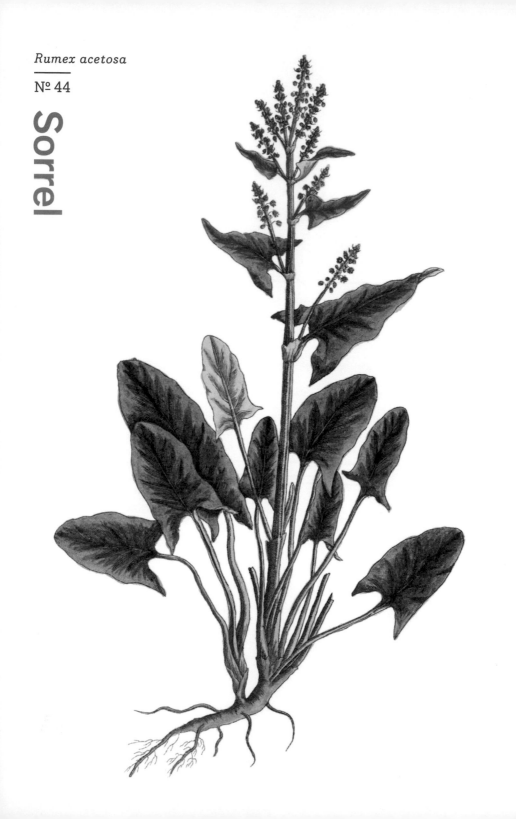

TO GROW

This hardy plant prefers full sun and well-drained soil. Begin with seeds or cuttings. Grows up to 3 feet and happily lives near strawberries in the garden. Can also be grown in containers. Keep moist and harvest leaves when they are young; you will get several harvests throughout the season.

USAGE

Leaves have a tart taste reminiscent of kiwi or wild strawberries. Add them to salad when young and fresh and be sure to mix in other greens to balance flavors. Most often found in sauces, stews, and soups. Complements fish dishes. Use on potatoes or omelets or make into pesto.

Various Indian curries include sorrel. In Afghanistan, leaves are dipped in a batter and deep-fried for a popular appetizer. Greeks mix sorrel with spinach and feta to make spanakopita. In Albania, simmered leaves are marinated and eaten cold or added to burek pies. The oxalic acid in sorrel means it should be eaten in moderation when raw; however, cooking the leaves greatly reduces the oxalic acid.

Sorrel is also called common sorrel, garden sorrel, narrow-leaved dock, and spinach dock. The perennial plant is in the same family as rhubarb and also has a sour taste. The transformation of the flowers' color makes the plant unique. In early summer they change from reddish-green to purple. Native to Europe and Asia, it is commonly found in grasslands and uncultivated, stony areas and should not be confused with the "sorrel of the Caribbean," or roselle (*Hibiscus sabdariffa*).

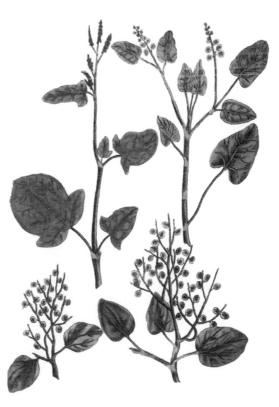

Egg-Lemon Soup with Sorrel

This silky soup gets additional bright lemon flavor from the sorrel, which also acts as a fresh green accent.

YIELD

Serves 4

6 cups vegetable broth
4 potatoes, peeled and chopped
3 large eggs
  Juice of 1 lemon (2 to 3 tablespoons)
1 cup sorrel leaves, cut crosswise into strips
  Salt and freshly ground pepper

In a large saucepan, bring the vegetable broth to a boil and add the potatoes.

Reduce the heat to low and simmer for 8 to 12 minutes, until the potatoes are cooked. Meanwhile, beat the eggs until frothy.

While continuing to whisk, slowly pour in about ½ cup of the hot broth, then add the lemon juice.

Remove the soup from the heat and gradually add the egg mixture, whisking constantly, for about 1 minute; the soup will thicken to consistency of light cream.

Stir in the sorrel and season to taste with salt and pepper.

Serve with toasted pita wedges.

Spearmint

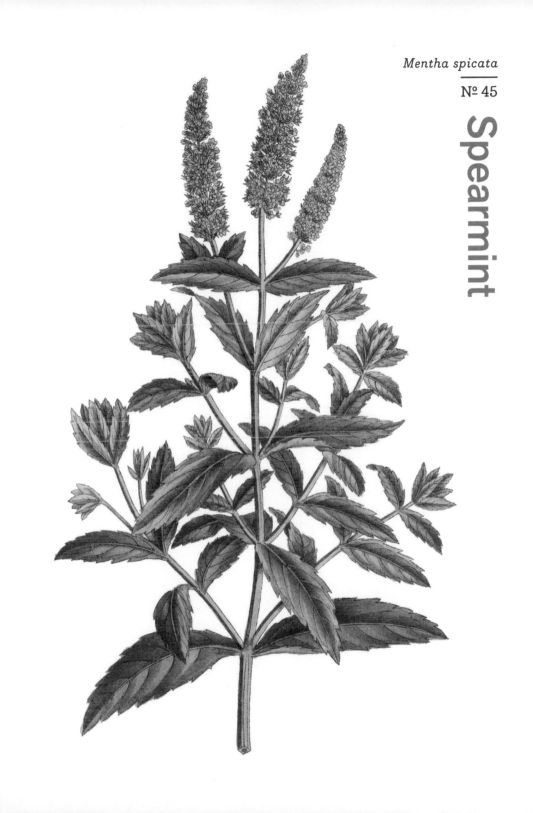

In the Victorian language of flowers, spearmint means warmth of sentiment.

TO GROW

In full sun and well-drained, moist soil, it will reach up to 3 feet. It spreads easily and therefore is often grown in containers. After flowering, the plant loses its fragrance.

USAGE

Leaves can be used in any form—fresh, frozen, or dried. Try combining it with basil in pesto; add to salads with watermelon and feta, or as a garnish for fruits and yogurts. Make a pasta with goat cheese, peas, lemon, parsley, and mint. Add to roasted parsnips or snap peas. It is a common accompaniment for lamb. Add to smoothies and ice cream. It's popular in mojitos and mint julep cocktails. Perhaps most commonly found in tea—iced and hot—and one of the key ingredients in Maghrebi or Moroccan mint tea. The flavoring is also found in toothpaste, mouthwash, shampoo, and chewing gum.

With bright green leaves and pink, white, or purple flowers, spearmint is also known as lamb mint, garden mint, mackerel mint, and common mint. Native to Europe and Asia, spearmint has a sweet, minty, pungent aroma and fruity taste. The perennial stands for welcome and hospitality in Morocco, where the bright green leaves are common in the mountains. The pointed leaves gave rise to the Latin species name, *spicata*, which translates to bearing a spike.

Pliny the Elder mentions spearmint, as does the Bible. The hardy perennial may have been used to clean teeth as far back as the fourteenth century. The Romans likely brought it to England. A sixteenth-century herbalist said spearmint could lift one's mood. The British did not tax the herb in the US colonies, making mint tea a favorite of the colonists.

Minty Bourbon Citrus Cocktail

Makes 1 cocktail

- **2** sprigs of spearmint
- **2** ounces bourbon
- **1½** ounces fresh orange juice
- **½** ounce fresh lime juice

In a shaker, muddle 1 sprig of mint until the leaves are bruised. Add the bourbon, orange and lime juices, and a handful of ice and shake well. Strain into a coupe glass and add the other mint sprig for garnish.

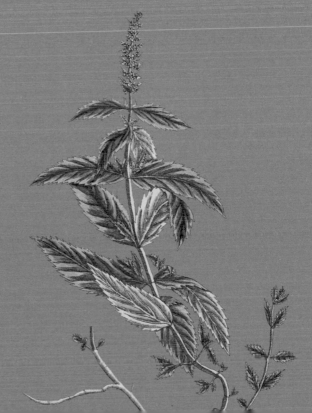

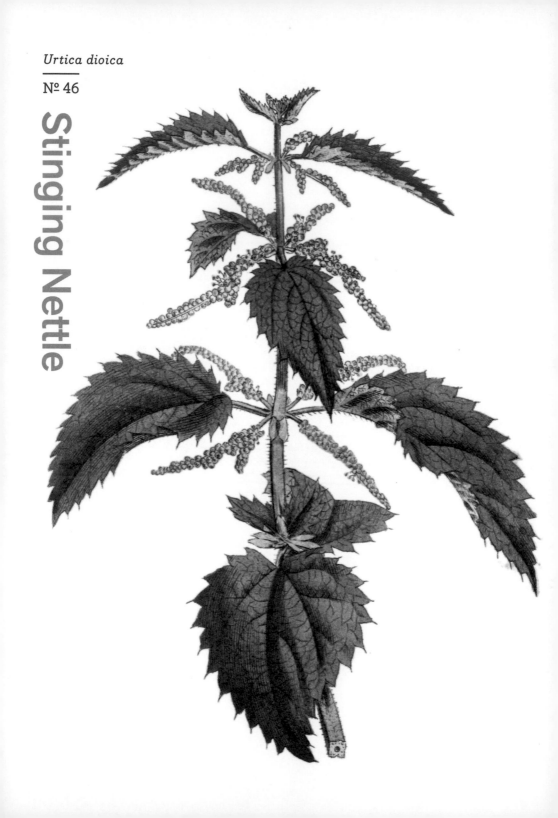

Urtica dioica

Nº 46

Stinging Nettle

In the Victorian language of flowers, stinging nettle symbolizes slander.

TO GROW

Preferring open areas or partial shade, nettles will grow to 6 to 8 feet. Thrive in moist soil and often found near rivers or streams, along roadsides, and in pastures and nurseries. The herbaceous plant spreads easily through rhizomes and is typically considered a weed. Nettles can be consumed but care must be taken with harvesting and preparing the plant. Wear gloves that protect your hands. For food or tea, pick before flowering. Young tops are best. To make the nettles safe for handling without gloves and eating, soak in water or cook.

USAGE

Tops are nutty; leaves have a peppery taste reminiscent of spinach. Nettles are most commonly found in soup or tea. Also used in nettle pudding, a vegetable dish made in the UK that dates back thousands of years. Can be added to Greek favorite spanakopita. Nettles have been used to make beer, wine, and Champagne. A treatment for thinning or damaged hair is made from nettles simmered in water. A linen-like fabric has been made from nettles for sheets, clothing, and sacks. Because nettle grows easily

This hardy perennial is also known as California nettle, slender nettle, tall nettle, or wild nettle. Native to Europe, it was brought to America by colonists and is often confused with Wood Nettle (*Laportea canadensis*), which is native to North America. Both nettles sting. Chemicals contained in the hairs on the stalk and leaves of stinging nettle can irritate the skin, leading to a burning or itching sensation. The genus name is derived from the Latin word *urere*, to burn.

without pesticides, it may be a useful eco-friendly alternative source of material. Nettle is also used to make green and yellow dye. Attracts butterflies to the garden and makes an effective fertilizer.

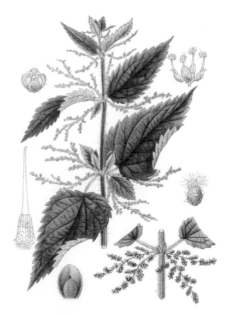

Nettle Hair Tonic

Nettles have also been used to prevent hair loss and promote hair growth. To make the hair tonic, you need 2 pints of water and a handful (use your gloves!) of young nettles.

Simmer for 2 hours. Remove from heat and let cool. When the mixture has cooled, strain into a glass jar and seal. After shampooing, comb the nettle juice through your hair to stimulate new growth and keep hair shining and healthy.

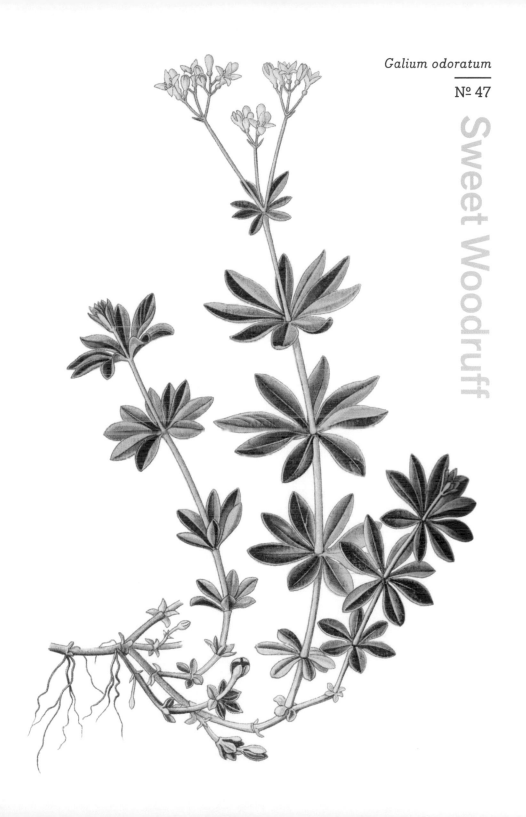

Sweet Woodruff

In the language of flowers, sweet woodruff symbolizes humility.

TO GROW

Grows well in shady areas with moist, well-drained soil. Provides nice ground cover and will grow up to 8 inches tall, needing little attention except watching that it doesn't spread too much. In summer, keep up with watering and harvest just before flowering. To dry, hang upside-down in a cool, dark spot.

USAGE

In Germany, woodruff has a long and celebrated history in beverages of all kinds. (The name in German, Waldmeister, means master of the woods.) Sweet woodruff is used to make May wine, a light wine drunk as part of a spring welcoming ceremony traditionally held on May 1. Berliner weisse beer is accompanied by a shot of green woodruff syrup. Some people pour it into Hefeweizen. Found in candies, syrups, jellies and cheesecake. Popular in potpourri, sachets, and dream pillows. Repels moths.

Sweet woodruff is one of the herbs that needs to wilt or dry out in order to develop its characteristic flavor. Note: One of the flavor compounds is coumarin, which is toxic in very high dosage. The

Also called sweet-scented bedstraw and master of the woods, woodruff is native the Middle East and Europe. The hardy perennial has white, star-shaped flowers. Crushing leaves releases a sweet smell often compared to fresh hay or sometimes vanilla. During the Middle Ages, the herb was a strewing herb and used in dry form to keep clothing, linens, and mattresses fresh. Woodruff pillows were valued at this time as it was believed the plant could help bring on sleep.

amount here is safe to drink, but should be avoided by people who are pregnant or lactating.

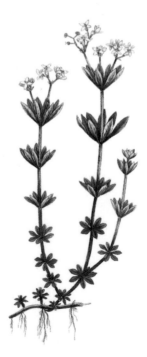

Mai-Wineless Punch

½ cup fresh-picked sweet woodruff leaves or
    1 heaping tablespoon dried woodruff (if using
    fresh woodruff leaves, wash them, let them
    dry, and leave them overnight to wilt; if using
    dried, infuse for no more than 30 minutes
    and strain)
2   quarts fresh apple cider
1   quart sparkling water
1   lemon, sliced thin
1   orange, sliced thin
    Optional: fresh flowering woodruff sprigs
    and/or sliced seasonal fruits, for garnish

In a large bowl, infuse the woodruff in the apple cider
for an hour or two for fresh leaves; 30 minutes for
dried, until fragrance develops. Strain the leaves out,
add sparkling water (you could also use sparkling
lemonade), sliced citrus, and ice to chill. Serve in glasses
garnished with fresh woodruff and/or seasonal fruits.

Artemisia dracunculus

№ 48

Tarragon

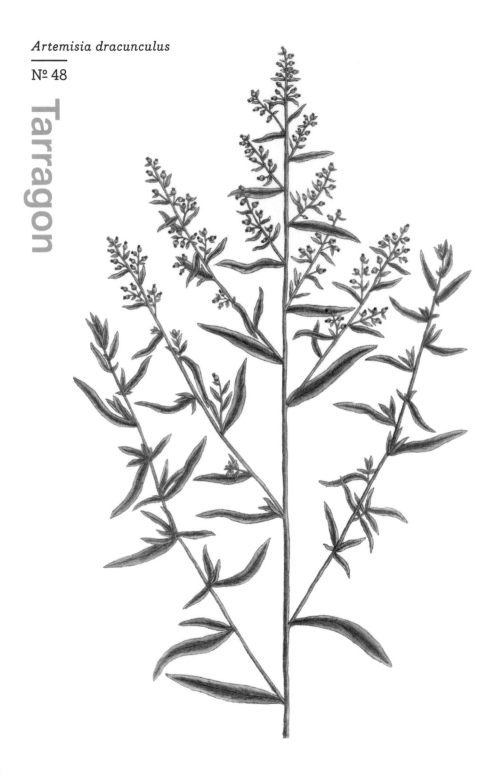

In the language of flowers, tarragon stands for lasting interest.

TO GROW

Tarragon can grow up to 5 feet. It prefers full sun and well-drained soil. It can be started with cuttings and will spread easily through roots. Fresh stems can be stored in water on the counter for up to 1 week. If you wash the stems and dry the cuttings thoroughly before storing, dried tarragon can last up to 1 year.

USAGE

Tarragon is one of the four *fines herbes* of French cooking, along with parsley, chives, and chervil. Steeping tarragon in vinegar is essential to a Béarnaise sauce, a favorite of French cuisine, and tarragon is used to make a classic Dijon mustard sauce with white wine and cream. It complements many chicken and fish dishes and is added to salads and omelets. For a unique dessert, try it in grapefruit sorbet. Tarragon is also used in a Russian soft drink called Tarkhuna. Iranian cuisine adds copious quantities to stews as well as pickles.

This small perennial native to Russia and Asia is also called mugwort, little dragon, and estragon. Tarragon has aromatic, needle-like leaves and a peppery taste. Its genus name pays tribute to the Greek goddess of the moon Artemis. The species name means small dragon, a possible reference to the strong taste or root shape. Another possible origin may have been the belief that it was an antidote to certain snake venoms. The most commonly grown type is French tarragon. Its strong taste resembles licorice thanks to the compound estragole, which is also found in fennel and anise. A milder taste but stronger plant variety can be found in Russian tarragon. Spanish tarragon, also known as Mexican mint marigold or winter tarragon, is a separate plant genus.

Tarragon Roasted Chicken Thighs

Serve this delicately flavored dish with brown rice or quinoa.

YIELD
—
4 servings

2	tablespoons olive oil
10	large shallots, peeled and quartered
2	pounds boneless, skinless chicken thighs
1	bunch tarragon
	Salt and freshly ground pepper
½	cup chicken broth
¼	cup dry vermouth

Preheat oven to 400 degrees.

Oil a baking sheet and add the shallots, tossing to coat with oil. Roast for 10 minutes, until softened. Remove the pan from the oven and add the chicken thighs to the pan. Scatter the tarragon over, and sprinkle with salt and pepper. Stir the chicken broth and vermouth together, then pour over the chicken. Roast until the chicken is cooked through (around 20 minutes). If the shallots and chicken are getting too brown, cover with a sheet of aluminum foil or parchment paper.

Thyme

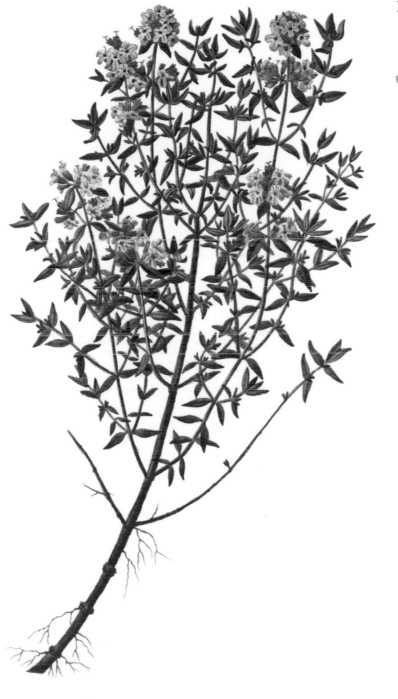

In the Victorian language of flowers, thyme stands for activity.

This small perennial is also called garden thyme, common thyme, French thyme, and German thyme. Native to the Mediterranean, it is a member of the mint family. It is a bit spicier in taste than its cousin oregano, and notes of lemon, orange, lavender, or coconut can be detected in some species. Flowers are small and either pink or purple.

TO GROW

Thyme grows 8 to 12 high inches and does well in full sun and well-drained soil. It can be easily grown from cuttings. Much of the characteristic flavor remains after drying, but you should strip the leaves from the stems before using.

USAGE

Thyme is part of the classic French collection of herbs called *bouquet garni* as well as the *herbes de Provence* mix. It is commonly used to flavor breads, soups, and stews and is delicious on roasted potatoes or carrots. Eggplant, lamb, and beef partner well with thyme. Thyme contains an antiseptic called thymol, an active ingredient in mouthwash and some skin care products. Because of its delicate flowers, many varieties are enjoyed as ornamental plants.

Thyme was important to ancient Egyptians for use in embalming. Ancient Romans believe thyme could offer protection from poison. To the Greeks, it was associated with courage and strength. Both Romans and Greeks used it in purification ceremonies. It was used as a sleep aid and to repel nightmares in the Middle Ages. Also in this period, it continued to represent bravery and was often carried into battle. The herb was believed to offer protection against the bubonic plague. For Victorians, finding thyme in the woods meant a fairy revelry had taken place in that patch.

Thyme Syrup

Thyme is an excellent expectorant as well as an antimicrobial herb, and honey not only soothes but is also a preservative. It can be used for colds, coughs, laryngitis, and sore throats.

Steep 1 ounce dried thyme leaves in 1 cup boiled water, covered, until cool, then strain. Mix the liquid with 1 cup honey. Store refrigerated in a glass jar. It keeps well for several months. Give undiluted doses of 1 teaspoon to 1 tablespoon several times a day as needed.

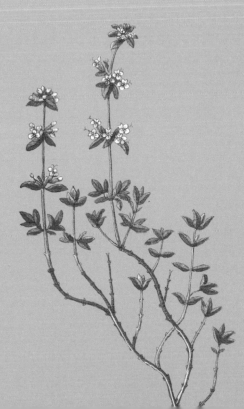

Viola sororia

№ 50

Wild Violet

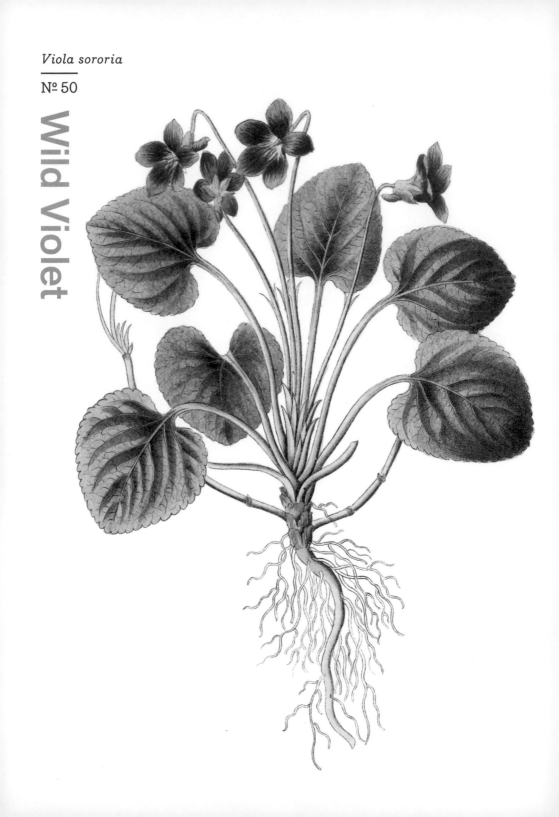

In the Victorian language of flowers, the white violet connotes modesty or innocence, whereas the purple violet conveys romantic love.

TO GROW

Violets grow well in moist, shady spots. They can spread easily through their runners. To grow, transfer wild plants into the garden. Harvest in spring and early summer.

USAGE

Leaves and flowers of the common blue violet are edible, and the plant is rich in vitamins A and C. The petals do not offer much flavor, but they make a colorful garnish for salads and punches. They can be used in syrups, jellies, and baked goods; when candied or crushed they lend their color to sugar. Flowers frozen in ice make a stunning addition to party drinks. Sweet violet is used in perfumes as well as flavorings for food and beverages.

There are between 500 and 600 species of violets, growing on all continents except Antarctica. Common names for viola species include heartsease, wild pansy, and Johnny jump-up. The common blue violet, native to most of North America, is such a familiar sight on lawns and sidewalks it is often considered a weed. Sweet violet, native to Europe and Asia, has fragrant dark purple flowers and is also known as wood violet or English violet.

Ancient Greeks used violets in perfume and adopted the flower as a symbol for Athens. The ancient Romans used it to make wine. For both cultures, it was associated with death. Napoleon also cherished violets, and covered his wife Josephine's grave with them. In Shakespeare's *Hamlet*, Ophelia says the violets died when her father passed away.

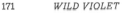

Crystallized Violets

These lovely candied blossoms gained popularity in Europe in the eighteenth century.

YIELD

Makes 20 candied violets

- **20** fresh-picked violets with stems on
- **1** egg white
- **1** tablespoon superfine or confectioners' sugar

Pick your flowers from areas that haven't been touched with pesticides or animals because you will not be rinsing them.

Beat the egg white until it is frothy but not stiff. Pick up a violet by its stem and dip the whole head into the egg white. Spin it gently to shake off the excess, then sprinkle with the sugar to coat it evenly. A sifter will help distribute it evenly.

Place the violets on a baking sheet lined with parchment and allow them to dry. As the flowers dry, most of the sugar will be absorbed by the egg white, creating a glaze on the petals. You can quicken the drying stage by leaving them in the oven with the light left on overnight. Once completely dry, snip off the stems and store for up to 6 months in an airtight jar.

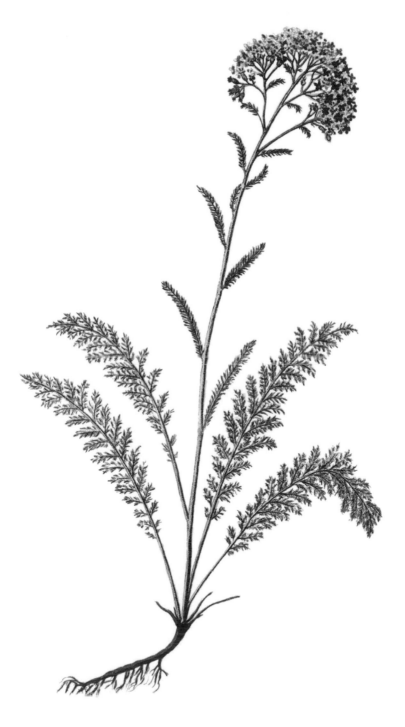

In the language of flowers, yarrow symbolizes both healing and everlasting love.

TO GROW

Yarrow likes full sun and well-drained soil. It tolerates drought and will grow 2 to 4 feet. Start from seed in early summer and plant ¼ inch into the dirt, spaced 1 to 2 feet apart. Yarrow spreads quickly. Harvest when the plant flowers. It will bloom white and pink flowers from April through September in some regions.

USAGE

Yarrow is popular for its ornamental beauty and is often enjoyed in garlands, at weddings, as groundcover in wildflower gardens, and in dried bouquets. But it is particularly valued for its medicinal properties. People continue to use it to treat burns and scrapes as a salve and to relieve symptoms of cold and flu as well as poor digestion. (Both leaves and flowers can be steeped as a tea.) The Cowlitz people use yarrow as a hair rinse; it is said to improve hair quality and enhance color. In Scandinavia it is used to brew beer and as a spice. The aromatic herb can be used as a mosquito repellent and will attract butterflies to the garden. Be aware, however, that yarrow may cause an allergic reaction and pregnant women should use it only under the supervision of a doctor.

This flowering perennial is part of the family Asteraceae. Native to Europe, Asia, and North America, yarrow is also called milfoil, bloodwort, the witch's herb, snake's grass, bad man's plaything, and devil's nettle. The genus name is said to originate with the warrior Achilles from Greek mythology who applied yarrow to the wounds of soldiers. The herb was used for actual soldiers as well and once called *herba militaris*—military herb—for that reason. The species name, "thousand leaved," refers to the feathery foliage. Dental evidence taken from scrapings of tooth tartar suggests that yarrow was used medicinally by Neanderthals. The Navajo people in North America consider yarrow a sacred "life medicine" and use it to treat fevers and headaches and as a salve for sores. Other native tribes, including the Pawnee and Chippewa, also rely on it for pain relief. In medieval times, yarrow was used to flavor ale, keep evil spirits away, and treat toothaches (a remedy that continued until the nineteenth century). Yarrow has been seen by many as having mystical properties. It has been used in spells, to foretell the future, and in chants of protection. The stalks are used in *I Ching* divinations in China dating from the Zhou dynasty 1046 BC to 249 BC.

Yarrow Bath

This wonderful infusion turns your bath into an oversize teacup.

Fill a muslin bag or a washcloth with fresh or dried yarrow flowers, close the bag, and secure with a rubber band. If you know of a safe place to pick fresh yarrow flowers, the activity of walking, seeking out the plant, and inhaling its flowers will be calming in and of itself and the bath will be a soothing treat.

Suspend the bag or washcloth from the bathtub's faucet so it soaks in the bathwater as the tub fills.

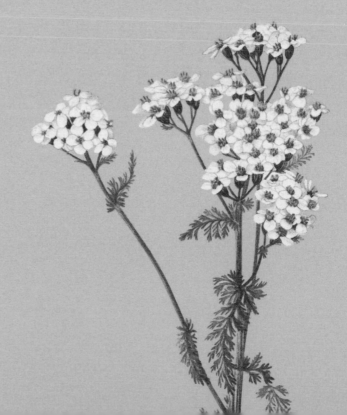

Published in the United States by Clarkson Potter/Publishers, an imprint
of Random House, a division of Penguin Random House LLC, New York.
clarksonpotter.com

CLARKSON POTTER is a trademark and POTTER with colophon is a
registered trademark of Penguin Random House LLC.

Library of Congress Cataloging-in-Publication Data
Names: New York Botanical Garden, author.
Title: Herbal handbook : 50 profiles in words and art from the archives
    of The New York Botanical Garden Herbal handbook / The New York
    Botanical Garden.
Other titles: Fifty profiles in words and art from the archives of The New York
    Botanical Garden
Description: New York : Clarkson Potter, [2022]
Identifiers: LCCN 2021015207 (print) | LCCN 2021015208 (ebook) |
    ISBN 9781524759131 (hardcover) | ISBN 9780593235683 (ebook)
Subjects: LCSH: Herbals. | Herb gardening. | Cooking (Herbs) | Herbs.
Classification: LCC SB351.H5 N47 2022 (print) | LCC SB351.H5 (ebook) |
    DDC 635/.7—dc23

ISBN 978-1-5247-5913-1
eISBN 978-0-593-23568-3

Printed in China

Botanical art supplied by NYBG
Editor: Lindley Boegehold
Designer: Danielle Deschenes
Production Editor: Serena Wang
Production Manager: Jessica Heim
Composition: Merri Ann Morrell and Nick Patton
Copy Editor: Anne Cherry

10 9 8 7 6 5 4

First Edition